At my French Table

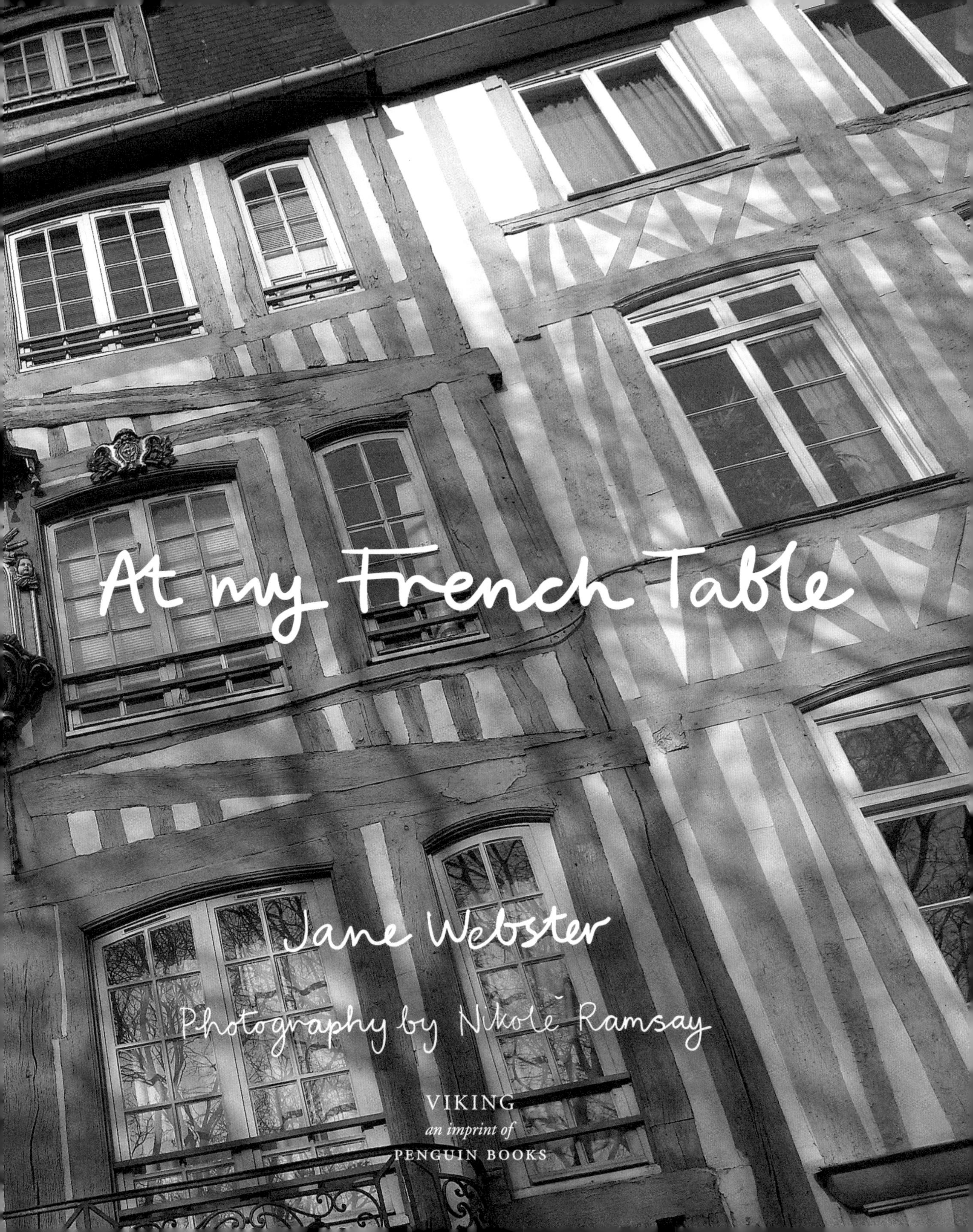

At my French Table

Jane Webster

Photography by Nikole Ramsay

VIKING
an imprint of
PENGUIN BOOKS

For Mum, who taught me how to dream,
and Pete, who makes my dreams come true

Contents

Château de Bosgouet, Normandy.

Le début
(the beginning)

Pourquoi? Why? This is often the first question that friends, family and even strangers ask me. Why uproot a perfectly happy family from their native Australia for an uncertain future in France? The first few times I was asked this I floundered and stammered, struggling to answer the question; how could I articulate something that had lain so deep in me for so long?

My husband, Peter, and I are Melburnians, but we've always liked to think of ourselves as Francophiles – even when we could hardly put a sentence together *en français*. Our first trip to France was in 1990 when we were on our honeymoon. Pete and I walked around the streets of Paris for hours each day, one of us squeezing the other's hand tight whenever we saw something breathtaking, which was often. It was the perfect start to our marriage. We were captivated by the cuisine in Paris, too. I had always had a great love of cooking. The reverential way in which the French treated food – using only the very best seasonal ingredients and taking the time needed to properly prepare them – made me feel as if I'd come home.

I also remember the two of us, noses pressed against the window on a TGV train travelling from Paris to Dijon, hoping for a tiny glimpse of a château through the forests. The French countryside was beautiful but I'll admit it: back then I was really a city girl. I was easily seduced by the impossible glamour of Paris and the effortless cool of her people. I didn't even put up a fight.

On returning to Australia from our honeymoon, I immediately signed on to a number of French cooking courses at The French Kitchen in Melbourne and the Lake House in Daylesford. My family and friends would good-naturedly try out all my creations. It was so gratifying to have them taste my *steak au poivre* or *tarte au citron* and get a contented, closed-eyed *Mmm* in response. That *Mmm* was my measure of success.

The reactions to my creations were encouraging enough to suggest that I could cook for a living. I continued my cooking courses and befriended a few of the chefs who ran them. They were equally encouraging. Eventually I resigned from my job as a primary school teacher to open a small café in Armadale, Melbourne. Thinking of the Paris train station, I called my café La Gare. In retrospect I'm surprised by my courage – I had no experience in the café trade, but it never occurred to me that this was a reason not to give it

Preparing baking moulds for baguettes in the village boulangerie.

baguette céréales 130 gr
1,25 €
5,43 € le Kg

baguette de St Ouen. 130 gr
1,10 €
4,78 € le Kg

...in à base de levain
...gr
1,90 €
...93 € le Kg

pain céréales
1,70 €
5,15 € le Kg

pain aux noix
330 gr
1,70 €
5,15 € le Kg

a go. Perhaps I was young and idealistic, but this approach paid off. Despite my boldness, I was keen to absorb as much I could from more experienced epicureans. Whenever I felt unsure of myself, I'd seek counsel from friends in the industry.

Each day I would spend hours cooking in the café's minute kitchen and serving the ladies of Armadale coffee and *pâtisseries* – tiny tastes of France. It seemed I had found an outlet for my passion, but during my time at the café I still daydreamed, envisaging our next trip to France.

The years passed. Pete and I were blessed with four wonderful kids: Lachlan, Millie, Madeleine and Alex. Meanwhile, my sister, Sallyanne, had fallen for a Belgian, Theo. To my great delight they settled in a village just outside Paris. I sternly told myself that it was my familial duty to visit them – often. So every year we would take the whole family on vacation to France; these visits were the start of my real education. I made it my mission to get to know the local foodie scene. I ate where native Parisians ate – away from the showy, overpriced tourist traps – and shopped where they shopped, making good use of the fresh-food markets. I gleaned as much information as I could from my culinary-minded Parisian friends about how to perfect the art of French home-style cooking, and took master classes with some of France's best chefs at the Ritz Hotel.

Our family's trips became longer and more frequent. We experienced more of the French countryside with each trip and would often find ourselves in the northwest corner of France, in Normandy. I was struck by the beauty of this region – its verdant farmlands, bustling markets and amazing regional produce – and by the generosity of its locals. Those châteaux also started to catch my eye again. Over time I became preoccupied with the idea of château life, of immersing my young family in the culture, language and

Some of my favourite places to shop in
the nearby village of Bourg-Achard.

Traditional half-timbered houses in Rouen,
the capital of Upper Normandy.

cooking of the French countryside. The idea of rural life coloured all that I saw, and it was the measure against which I judged everything else. Back in Melbourne, our small inner-city herb garden seemed to be bulging at the seams. Our house seemed cramped and confining. City life now seemed alienating. I felt an intense longing for the space and freedom that rural life promised.

With every trip we inched closer to making the big decision – staying in France for a longer period of time – but we had no real reason to take this next step. Then in 2003 a daring dream entered my head: it was the seed of a business idea. I was sure that there were plenty of people like me out there – people who shared my love of French cuisine and culture, people who wanted an insider's view of the foodie scene. But I was well aware that in France you couldn't go 5 metres without tripping over someone running a gourmet tour. I didn't want to be one of the flock who waved in the direction of a couple of quaint shopfronts and bought everyone a *café crème* at the end of the day; I'd have to distinguish myself. I mused that while I always enjoyed traipsing around fresh-food markets and dining in out-of-the-way restaurants, what really thrilled me was rolling up my sleeves and trying out recipes myself. *This* was my eureka moment: I could run culinary tours combined with hands-on cooking classes.

It was clear that this sort of experience would be best suited to a provincial area. Indeed, this would be the appeal: I could offer my guests a chance to experience the charm of French rural life, while introducing them to the region's cuisine. It would be a gastronome's perfect vacation!

I smiled to myself. Approached the right way, the venture could also give our family the opportunity to opt out of our Melbourne life for a while. We could escape the wheel of long work hours, appointments and kids'

extra-curricular activities, and at the same time I could share my knowledge and experience with like-minded people.

The idea started to take shape. I would entice the great chefs I had worked with over the years to teach my guests the intricacies of French cooking, while I would play hostess – cooking the guests' day-to-day meals and organising their itineraries.

I would run these gastronomic holidays over the European summer when the weather and produce were at their best. I suspected I would need a year or two to ground myself in France, to really get to know the region I would be showing off and to set up the business side of things. I could return to France each summer to continue the tours. Who wouldn't want an excuse to escape the dreary Melbourne winter for a few weeks each year? I even thought of a name for my budding business: The French Table – catchy, *non?*

The more I thought about this, the more tempting the proposition became. I talked it over with Pete, who supported the idea entirely. In fact, there were times when he seemed even more smitten with the venture than I was. We reasoned that for the business to be successful we'd need to buy a place large enough to comfortably accommodate our family and The French Table guests. We would also need enough room for a commercial-sized kitchen for the cooking classes. In short, we'd need a house the size of a palace, or at least the size of a château. Pete and I had no illusions about this being a long-term, risky endeavour that would require a substantial investment of both our time and money, but for reasons of optimism, naïvete or madness we were willing to chance it.

In October 2003 Pete and I put our businesses on hold and pulled the kids out of school for the term so we could look for a place to live in France. The children were behind the idea of moving to France and living in a castle for

Le début 13

Our (eventual) French sitting room.

a couple of years. There was the odd revolt; Lachie began to wonder just how much he might miss his Melbourne school friends, but for the most part we were all on the same page – excited about what lay ahead. Before we left, we lined up a number of real-estate appointments. We were keen on the idea of staying close to Paris and London, and Normandy fit the bill perfectly. Its geographical benefits were bolstered by its gastronomical ones – it's a food lover's paradise.

We were interested in a château for sale in the village of Bosgouet – population 480 – only 25 kilometres from the city of Rouen, the capital of Haute-Normandie (Upper Normandy). Bosgouet is tiny: its centre is made up of only a two-roomed school house, *la mairie* (the mayor's office) and a church. Château de Bosgouet sits on a park in the middle of the village.

The first time we went to see Château de Bosgouet we got hopelessly lost on the way. By the time we found it, we were two-and-a-half hours late for our rendezvous with Monsieur Michel, the real-estate agent. Monsieur had missed his lunch and was looking less than impressed when we pulled up in our rented Renault Espace. As our four rather dishevelled children tumbled out of the car, the poor man must have wondered what he had struck – we looked more like a travelling circus than prospective buyers. Pete and I politely made our apologies. Monsieur Michel extricated the château's huge wrought-iron gates from their tangle of chain and padlock, then led us onto the property. Down the long driveway a red-and-white château sat amid a park of grand old trees.

Our children are generally cheerful château visitors, but they become less eager participants when their tummies are empty. On this particular day they had not eaten anything since breakfast. They ran around madly in the long grass, and I nervously warned them to watch out for snakes. While poor Pete

tried to get the kids to calm down, I glanced around at the château and its expansive grounds. The shutters on the dozens of windows were closed hard; the gardens were rambling and unkempt.

We followed Monsieur Michel into the château. Pete went first with camera in hand, as always, capturing every detail. Following closely behind him were Lachlan, Millie, Madeleine and lastly Alex. Our rumbling tummies meant that the tour would have to be the short version. I was only too aware that mutiny would erupt if we did not feed the hungry troops soon. My eyes darted from one room to the next, taking in as much as I could in the time we were there. I managed to retain the important facts like, yes, there were oak parquetry floors and marble mantelpieces in excellent condition, and although every surface of the château was filthy, there weren't any obvious structural problems. To my eyes all that would be needed to make it shine was some interior-decorating nous and a slightly daunting amount of elbow grease.

I was thrilled when I saw a huge commercial kitchen in the basement – rugged stainless steel with all the fittings a cook could want, and what's more, it had hardly been used. *It would be perfect for my cooking school*, I thought gleefully. When Michel informed us that the owners were taking the kitchen fittings because they had already lined up a buyer for them, I shrugged and heaved in the customary French way, saying that it was a great pity. We ended the visit with Pete keen, but me not so sure – such a shame about that wonderful kitchen!

After the tour, Michel departed swiftly, his mind no doubt on his overdue lunch. We six sat in our car at the rear of Château de Bosgouet and picnicked on baguettes, cheese and thick slices of the ripe tomatoes we had bought that morning from the local village market. We finished the meal with some delicious pastries – pithiviers jammed full of sautéed mushrooms and shallots – washed down with large mugfuls of steaming hot chocolate. Nourished but nowhere near certain about the château, we slowly pulled away from our picnic spot with fogged-up windows and loads to think about.

Our second visit to the château a week or two later was more enlightening than the first. This time Michel gave us a little of its history. The Napoleonic-style Château de Bosgouet is considered young by European standards. It was built in 1853 on the foundations of a sixteenth-century château that had burnt to the ground some thirty years before. The five-storey château sits within a 50-acre park and has many outbuildings, some of which were used as servants' quarters. The château was occupied by the Germans during the Second World War and two rather unremarkable outbuildings were built on the grounds to accommodate the troops. One was used as sleeping quarters and the other built as a mess hall. Only those with rank and seniority could have ever expected to see the inside of Château de Bosgouet.

As he rattled off facts about the château's previous owners, Michel threw open the shutters of the floor-to-ceiling French windows. The sun streamed into the grand salons and reception rooms, making the parquetry floor look warm despite its obvious filth. Michel went on to show us each of the five floors, the outbuildings, and the remnants of a walled kitchen garden that looked ripe for renovation and cultivation. Again, our tour passed in a blur – overwhelming and overawing. With me still ruminating over whether it was the right place for us, we bid Michel farewell and promised to call him as soon as possible with our decision.

We sped off in the Espace, with me behind the wheel and Pete furious at his indecisive wife. I suggested that some lunch might aid negotiations. A decent meal and a tipple of good wine always mellows my husband's

Cherubs sit above the mantelpieces in the dining room at Château de Bosgouet.

The parquetry staircases in the two towers of the Château took weeks of work to restore.

mood, and so we sought out Auberge Saint-Michel, a pretty little restaurant hidden away on a back road in Lower Normandy. Our children are seasoned restaurant goers and appreciate good food as much as any adult foodie I know. Happily, in French restaurants children are always welcome and treated the same as adult customers. Our hostess Sophie kindly said she would create a special four-course menu for the children, starting with an aperitif of *citron pressé* (a sweetened fresh lemon juice), served with a plate of tiny cheesy puffs. It certainly stimulated the appetites of our four little gourmands. Their entrée was a beautifully composed salad of watercress – that French favourite! – tomatoes, goat's cheese and fresh herbs. This was followed by a perfectly cooked fillet of chicken with a typically Norman creamy mushroom sauce and freshly made tagliatelle on the side. We sat talking for hours, revived by our meal, but still no closer to making a decision.

I began to fret that I was taking my family on a track to disaster. Everyone was trusting my judgement and following my dream, but I was losing my nerve. What if my business idea didn't work out as I'd hoped? Might we founder without the grounding of the work and school lives we were used to? We left France at the end of 2003 to come back to Australia – no contract signed and no closer to moving.

We spent a few months in limbo. Each night Pete and I would take a walk together around the back streets of Armadale. On these walks our conversation would always come back to the topic of France. We'd either reminisce about our trips or endlessly catalogue the pros and cons of living in France. On Easter Sunday in 2004, during one of these walks, it hit me: *I don't want to wake up when I'm seventy-five and wish that we had done this*. I shared my thought with Pete and knew that I had struck a chord. This turned out to be the decisive moment. The idea that we would spend the rest of our marriage dreaming and talking about an adventure we would never embark on scared the living daylights out of us. Plus, we knew how much our whingeing about it would eventually bore our friends.

We got on the phone as soon as we could. Luckily Château de Bosgouet was still on the market and Monsieur Michel was most happy to hear from us. The kitchen that I had so admired became a bargaining chip in our negotiations. We said to Michel that the sale was conditional on the commercial kitchen staying with the château. I'd need a kitchen large enough to accommodate ten or so people comfortably in order for the cooking school to be a success; such an asset was not going to be easily replaced. We were quite prepared to lose the château if the kitchen was not going to be part of the sale. Luckily we prevailed; the kitchen would stay put.

Purchasing property in France is not an easy exercise; it is a lengthy and at times maddeningly complex process. The bureaucracy we encountered was by turns farcical and tedious. The laws that apply to the purchase of a property depend on the type of property you're buying. A vineyard or farm will be subject to different procedures and costs to that of a village house or a château. Every time we thought we had a handle on the laws we would unearth some ancient decree that shifted the goalposts yet again. Under French law every property that is on the market can be bought at the asking price by the village mayor on behalf of the townspeople. At one stage it looked as if this was going to happen with Bosgouet. The mayor decided that while he could not afford the whole property, he was keen on snapping up one of the château's outbuildings, the *maison de gardien* (caretaker's house) as a new library for the village school. This led to seemingly interminable negotiations between real-estate agents and notaries and international property lawyers. Then the mayor had a change of heart. Perhaps the village needed *two*

Prix
Produit
Variété
Origine
Calibre
Catégorie
Veloute
5€95

buildings for its school library? More in-depth consultations were needed, and no one seemed fussed about doing anything swiftly. It is an understatement to say that this was starting to get us down.

The mayor's indecision about which parts of the property he wanted and his leisurely deliberation as to whether the village could actually afford them was playing havoc with our lives. By this time it was clear that we were not going to arrive in France on the date we had expected. This added another complication. We had already organised to rent our Melbourne home to a family who was returning from London, and they were due to arrive and move into our house shortly.

We ran into more problems when the French government would not issue visas for our kids until the village school had accepted them as students – but the school would not accept our children until we were issued with visas. I went a bit cross-eyed at that one. After dealing with these dramas for many months, we were sorely tempted to call off the entire project. It took innumerable drawn-out conversations in my unpolished French, the aid of a crack team of Melbourne solicitors and bullish determination, but we finally triumphed. The mayor purchased half an acre of the château's land, on which he planned to build a new library; the London family ended up making an offer to buy our house, which we gratefully accepted; and our visas were issued without further grief.

All that was left was to pack up our lives in Melbourne, decide which of our possessions would travel with us and which would have to go into storage, and get on a plane back to France. After much deliberation we shipped over two 40-foot containers with almost all of our furniture inside, reasoning that the château was a very big property and could do with as much furniture as possible. I had also read that in big moves like this it was often

Friends and family around the table.

Lachlan

Millie

Alex

Madeleine

Me

Pete

much easier for children to be surrounded by familiar objects. We would take everything with us and start again once we returned to Melbourne.

We left Melbourne in late 2005. We would stay in France for a little under a year and a half, then return to Australia in time for the 2007 school year. I would use this time to set up my business, ready for my first group of guests. The children were aged twelve, eleven, nine and four when we left. It was a make or break time in terms of their education. Looking back, I believe we just made it, squeezing through a small window of opportunity. They were still wide-eyed and full of the adventurous spirit that would help them acclimatise to the French life and language.

Our nervous wait at Melbourne airport ended with a too-chipper boarding call for our flight. As we stepped onto the plane, I gave Pete's hand a squeeze and took in a deep breath. Who knew what would greet us on the other side of the world?

L'arrivée
(the arrival)

As the bedside alarm clock sounded, I stretched until I reached a state that passed for consciousness. First light at Bosgouet was worth getting up for. I watched out my window as the countryside was slowly illuminated. The fields, dotted with blossoming apple trees and marked out by hedgerows, were awash with early-morning pinks. This was Normandy in spring, and although I'd seen this spectacular exhibition many times since we'd arrived, I still needed a hard pinch or two to make sure I was not imagining it.

For months after our winter arrival in Normandy these daybreak starts had been vital – there was much work to be done. I'd realised immediately that we wouldn't be able to move directly into the château. The property had previously been used by the Romanville council as a *commune de vacances* (holiday camp) during the summers. But the place had been unoccupied since the council had given up its tenancy eight years ago. The intervening years had seen the château fall into disrepair, and every surface was thickly coated in oily dust. Worse still, we discovered that the château's once-elegant reception rooms had been stripped of their marble mantelpieces just prior to our arrival. The thieves removed our ten fireplaces, smashing walls in the process and leaving a ghastly mess behind them. This was a terrible blow, not least because the clean up was such an arduous job.

We spent that first winter in one half of another château ten minutes down the road, while we contemplated how best to tackle the job of cleaning up Château de Bosgouet. Our immediate plans were to scrub every wall and ceiling with sugar soap to prepare them for painting; clean the hundreds of French windows, inside and out; painstakingly wash the fine plasterwork on the walls of the ground floor; track down replacement fireplaces and tackle the parquetry floors, removing the inches of grime that covered them. I foolishly assured myself that washing away years of neglect would be extremely therapeutic. By the end of the first exhausting week of 'therapy' we knew we needed help.

In bygone days the château would have been overrun with domestic and outdoor staff. We hired three people to help with the day-to-day running of the place. They would stay on at the property after we'd gone back to Australia, taking care of things between our visits. New Yorker Paul, the wonderfully versatile caretaker whose expertise extended to plumbing and

Practising French with a new friend in the village.

1KG
Prix
Produit   Chou
Variété
Origine   Fran

L'arrivée 41

Tackling the parquetry floor with a tea-soaked cloth.

electrical work, lived at the edge of the estate. New Zealander Tim, the groundskeeper, lived in the gardener's cottage with his wife Angela and their three children. Chrystelle, our *femme de ménage*, who was housekeeper for a number of different households in the area, had worked at our château on and off since she left school in her teens. She had lived in the village of Bosgouet her entire life. Chrystelle is a woman of generous proportions, with a mouth to match – one which, I am told, gets her in all sorts of trouble in the village, where she has a reputation as the local gossip.

Everyone stoically pitched in with the mammoth task of cleaning the château. There is nothing like kneeling together in thick grime to help the bonding process. I was surprised that everyone's good spirits held up. There were times when I'd step out of whichever room we were working on to stare down the length of the château's corridors, counting the rooms on that floor we had yet to tackle – the number almost always exceeded that of my fingers. My shoulders would slump when I realised how much more labour there was ahead of us, but just at the point of despair, I'd hear the kids' giggles echoing through the empty rooms, or Tim would make a silly joke. These moments were great for reviving me, and I'd come at those grimy walls with renewed verve.

Cleaning the oak parquetry floors proved to be an arduous task. My first consultations were conducted with Chrystelle in my limited French. I had my own ideas about how the floors should be tackled: on hands and knees with the aid of a soft muslin cloth. I had heard that dipping the cloth in a bucket of boiling water that had been steeped with tea (loose-leaf tea tied in another square of muslin and dropped in the bucket) worked wonders on oak. Traditionally the muslin cloth is drenched in tea and then wrung out tightly so as to be just damp. Working on one panel at a time is best. Chrystelle looked on with bemusement and stomped off with mop and broom under one formidable arm and a brute of a commercial vacuum cleaner under the other. In the end my approach, though much more labour intensive, had far better results.

Stage two of my method required the floors to be rubbed with a concoction of equal parts turpentine and linseed oil. I made up the mixture in clean jam jars, vigorously shaking the contents as if making a salad dressing. This process of the restoration was the most satisfying: as we rubbed the contents of the jam jars into the floors, the rich, warm colours of the old oak came back to life.

After the turps and linseed oil had dried, the floors were then built up with liquid wax, which is used in homes all over France. Again I preferred the hands-and-knees method for a superior finish. Armed with an MP3 player loaded with my favourite music, it beat going to the gym!

By early spring the marathon cleaning sessions were out of the way. We could finally move in. I began to settle in to life at the château and in the village.

The sense of urgency that had choked our Melbourne lives vanished. Instead of the mad morning dash to get everyone off to school and work – hurriedly making lunches, taming the children's delinquent hair, ensuring everyone was wearing matching shoes – Pete and I practised the fine art of the linger. A stretch all too easily turned into an extra hour in bed. Of course there were still children to be gently shaken awake and breakfasts to be made, but there were no school uniforms to iron and no one in Normandy has ever heard of a lunch box. The children chose their own outfits and were treated to a delicious four-course lunch every day at school. There was no traffic to battle as *les enfants* walked down the driveway and just around the corner to

attend the village school. They were always accompanied by Pepi, the scruffy little schnoodle we dragged with us from the other side of the world.

That spring I spent time acquainting myself with the basement kitchen, getting to know its quirks. We took early morning bike rides and long family lunches. There were garden beds to plan, the region's markets to track down, local produce to take advantage of, and the fundamentals of the business to establish. By far the most taxing endeavour was getting my French up to par.

I had only just known enough French to get me through my stays in Paris. I was determined to become more fluent, and this was both an exhilarating and frustrating endeavour. Annik, my tutor, showed extraordinary patience in teaching me French vocab, grammar and pronunciation. We had intensive one-on-one lessons, but it was still slow going. I also attended informal conversation classes in the village, where the other participants were mainly mothers of kids who attended the village school. We would spend one hour speaking in English and another speaking in French. Inevitably we veered away from the material prescribed by our textbooks and sometimes these sessions were closer to gossip-fests than anything else. I reasoned that this didn't undermine the virtue of the exercise. The classes were an excellent way of getting to know my neighbours and friendships formed as we talked about our children and the school.

I pinned lists of verb conjugations all over the château and diligently recited these forms while preparing dinner – in time with cutting the vegetables. I often spent time at night making a list of the phrases I would need for the following day's chores and I *never* left the house without my dictionary. Quickly rustling through the dictionary's pages to find a word that had evaporated from my memory was much easier than relying on elaborate hand gestures to get across my message. And the people to whom I was talking

The market in the port town of Honfleur.

seemed to appreciate the effort, too. I'd get encouraging nods from my fellow villagers and they would always slow down their French to something just below warp-speed and try to straighten out their heavy regional accents. I got a thrill when chatting with newfound friends *en français*. The slow process of learning the language was characterised by an accumulation of tiny victories, but when I had my first dream in French I knew I was really on my way.

We were viewed quizzically by many locals – what business could a gang of unruly Australians have in a place like Bosgouet? No doubt they rolled their eyes at yet more foreign *bons vivants* trying to get a taste of French country life, but we did our best to fit in. We shopped in the next village and used local tradespeople. We asked for help when we needed it and in return offered to help our neighbours. I taught English to the children in the village school and techno-whiz Pete helped locals who had computer problems. These things helped with our assimilation into village life. We settled into a comfortable and happy coexistence with the people of Bosgouet – one based on mutual respect and burgeoning friendship.

The kids started to settle in at the village school, where not one word of English was spoken by either the teachers or pupils. Our four little Australians bravely faced up to the challenge and muddled through with giggles and charades. Every morning they left the house with broad smiles and every evening they related amusing anecdotes to Pete and me, laughing at their mistakes or thrilled at the progress of emerging friendships: 'Maxime gave me his email address today,' or, 'I asked Ruby if she would like to come over to play this weekend,' and then, 'I got an invitation to Alicia's birthday party!'

Alex at the village school.

The Bosgouet schoolhouse – just a hop, skip and a jump from the château.

The churchyard in the nearby town of Flancourt.

54 L'arrivée

Château life

Life at Bosgouet was marked not only by the obvious challenges of reconciling linguistic and cultural differences, but also by the quirks of living in a grand old house. It was easy to slip away unseen to a sunlit corner to read or muse about what I might cook for our next meal, but there were times when the sheer size of the château could be infuriating. Pete and I thought we would go absolutely mad trying to call the children for dinner. They were always off somewhere in a far wing of the château, or outside riding their bikes, collecting chestnuts, making movies or building their latest cubby house in one of the small *bois* (woods) that flank the grounds. We reinstated a huge wrought-iron bell attached to one of the château's towers. A decent tug on the chain attached to the bell's clapper elicits a satisfying sound – deep and plangent. Using a bell to summon the kids for dinner sometimes felt a little medieval, but it was the most effective method we came across.

There were also significant challenges in trying to keep a house this size clean. Each day there were bathrooms to be scrubbed, parquet to be waxed, windows to be cleaned, gardens to be tended, and laundry to be ironed and delivered to the many bedrooms scattered throughout the five floors. Thankfully the children doubled as couriers, taking their clothes from the pigeon-holes in the basement to their *chambres* (bedrooms) on the upper floors.

It was amazing how quickly a house the size of Bosgouet began to feel normal as familiar furniture filled the cavernous spaces and we settled into routines. Although there was a certain strangeness in conducting the most ordinary of family activities in such a grand setting, it is fair to say that after a few months the château didn't seem quite so imposing.

We found this untarnished painting of a courting scene on our bathroom tiles.

A spare bedroom—ready for one of our many guests.

Even as the novelty of the experience faded a little, crossing the château's threshold still took my breath away. The ground floor of the château is elevated and arrived at by ascending a flight of stone steps. This floor consists of four huge reception rooms, one opening up into the next through solid-panelled floor-to-ceiling doors that look like part of the walls once they're closed. The ornate plasterwork on the walls of each room tell their own stories. The *entrée* (entrance room) depicts figures of wild boars, rabbits and deer, their heads poking out from behind plaster foliage and *forêt* (forest), creating a tableau of that favourite French pastime, *la chasse* (the hunt).

To the right of the *entrée* is the salon. It has a (newly installed) majestic white fireplace and classic 14-foot French windows that overlook the front park. I wanted the room to have a homey and comfortable feel despite its grandness, so I decorated it with white couches, vivid silk carpets and piles of books. We used each room as a private retreat, but for large parties or formal receptions we opened up the doors to create an expanse. The ground floor houses the *salle à manger*, a formal dining room painted in duck-egg blue. The dining room has its original gilding intact on the panels and cornices and plump, gilded angels playing on their flutes keep watch over our diners.

This level also holds a study, Lachie's bedroom in the east corner, two powder rooms and a small kitchen affectionately known as 'the office'. The office has an unfussy stainless-steel oven and cook top, dishwasher, butler's sink, and room for a refrigerator and microwave. The reception levels of châteaux the size of Bosgouet will often house these kinds of small 'butler's kitchens'. They are traditionally used when only the immediate family are in residence. At Bosgouet it was not too often that we were alone. That year we had a great number of Australian visitors – we never knew we had so many friends! The practicality of this petite kitchen, complete with a dumb waiter

going down to the main scullery in the basement, made it perfect for breakfast preparation, or for making a quick pot of tea when guests unexpectedly called. I always used the office to prepare hors d'oeuvres and aperitifs when they were to be taken inside the château. The intimacy of the office made it my favourite place to cook for my family or a small dinner party.

An oak parquetry staircase with a wrought-iron balustrade leads up to the main bedrooms on the next floor of the château. The polished wooden floors are covered with a richly coloured *tapis* (rug) bought from a travelling carpet salesman who fortuitously wandered down the driveway one day. There are six king-size bedroom suites on this floor and rooms for the rest of the family.

The next floor has three huge dormitory-style bedrooms, with neat lines of single beds decorated with pretty French quilts, dressed in red-and-white toile, folded at each bed's end. These rooms proved worth their weight in gold whenever we had large house parties or played host to many families holidaying together. Bedside tables with individual lamps allowed us to accommodate large numbers of people without having to institute a boarding house-style policy of 'lights out'. On this level there is also a vast room with a high-beamed roof that we fitted out with a ping-pong table, TV, DVD player and lots of boardgames to keep everyone amused. The sheer size of the château meant that living with great throngs of people was not as chaotic as it might otherwise have seemed. There was always some way for you to find a private spot for yourself.

Halfway down the corridor on the fourth level there's another staircase that rises up to the top floor of the house: the attic. The attic was cleared and cleaned, painted and rid of the debris left by the previous owners, but in all honesty I couldn't see us ever using or needing more space! The children immediately made good use of it, though, and it was elaborately dressed up as the set for many of their homemade movies.

The basement, which actually sits at ground level, is the nerve centre of the château. We are fortunate that it's a light and airy space, with excellent views of the grounds – the perfect place to work. The basement houses my pride and joy: the commercial-sized kitchen that I was so taken with on our first visit. From the first I cooked out of this kitchen whenever we had guests. The walls of the kitchen are covered in white Italian tiles, broken only by the four sets of French windows.

Life at the château was arranged around this kitchen and its two smaller cousins, the adjacent scullery and the office upstairs. Everyone has heard the old chestnut 'the kitchen is the heart of the home', and although a bit hack-neyed, there's some truth to it. The basement kitchen was well equipped – boasting Rosières stainless-steel commercial-quality equipment – but it lacked a soul, a warm, inviting feeling. The enormous preparation bench looked particularly unfriendly. This was rectified by replacing the steel bench-top with a slab of white marble, and covering it

In the basement kitchen preparing lunch.

with earthenware jugs full of freshly picked herbs and wicker baskets full of fruit. The mammoth stove no longer looked quite so off-putting with a row of beaten copper pots sitting above it. The kitchen at Bosgouet underwent many changes that spring. It slowly evolved into a space in which we all loved to cook, chat, gather, read, paint, knit and plan.

The basement has a separate self-contained apartment that has traditionally been used as a residence for the château's caretaker, when there is one in residence. The basement also houses a linen room, which was dominated by a 20-foot long pine ironing table. When we first saw it the wood looked very thirsty, so I spent an afternoon rubbing beeswax into its surface; it came up beautifully. We would have loved to have relocated this wonderful relic to the reception level to use as a library table, but we lacked the advanced geometric skills needed to work out how to get it upstairs without significantly damaging the table, the stairwell or our patience. It became a brainteaser for those who visited us, and all furrowed their brows before inevitably throwing up their hands in frustration, declaring the task impossible. One of our guests cheerfully offered to aid the project by sawing the table in half. Dismayed at the idea, we decided to just keep it downstairs. We moved the table into a huge room in the southeastern corner of the basement where it catches the dappled light that comes through the window.

The basement also accommodates the laundry, a boot room, a workshop that most handypeople would kill for, as well as a wine cellar for Pete's 'babies'. These wines were thoughtfully chosen then brought home to be duly pondered over, turned and admired, as if they were great masterpieces. Pete scrupulously recorded their addition to the family in his journal before finally putting them to bed in his meticulously organised *cave*.

The cellar leads into a small room that we did not discover until several weeks into our residence. The children refer to it rather alarmingly as 'the

Maddie gets a treat
from Ladurée,
the famous
Parisian
pâtisserie.

Finding fireplaces

The château's original fireplaces were really superb pieces. We were devastated when we discovered they had been ripped out of our walls and stolen just before we arrived. We took weekly trips to les Puces, *the Paris flea markets*, to try to find replacements big enough to fit the massive holes that were now in our walls. We had no luck there. Then we began to buy the weekly publication put out by *L'Hôtel Drouot*, the famous antique auction house situated in Paris that organises superb auctions all over France. Our *Gazette-Drouot* became our bible and we scoured its pages for months. We did spot a few good examples, but all were priced over €80 000! Given that we had ten mantelpieces to replace, we knew that we'd have to try another tack. We eventually sourced some quality marble reproductions, which now sit snugly in our walls.

panic room'. It is a secure room lined with shelves – the perfect place for storing all our travel documents and filing cabinets. We have been informed in hushed tones by several elderly villagers that under this room is a passageway, a relic of the original sixteenth-century château, leading from Château de Bosgouet to *la mairie*, the mayor's office. It has also been said that at the end of the Second World War, German officers hid from the allies in this secret passageway, but none was ever known to have come back out again. One day we may uncover the entry that leads to the passage – but no bones, we hope. For now, though, it features heavily in the kids' ghost stories.

Two towers, which flank the body of the château, run from the basement right up to the fourth floor. Blessedly their staircases are made of the same rich oak as the floors. These stairs are the main access to all the floors. They were not dubbed 'the stairmasters' for nothing: they were murder on the thighs of all the inhabitants of Bosgouet. The circular walls of the towers soon served as a gallery for Australian paintings and prints, providing guests with a good excuse to stop and stretch their limbs before persevering.

There are enough outbuildings and cottages on the estate to mean that it will likely be many years before we are short of a project. The most impressive of the outbuildings is the red-brick stables that date back to the sixteenth century. The stables have boxes for six horses, a tack room and accommodation for the stable-hands. A local gentleman, Monsieur Christophe, wanted to agist his horses in our stables in exchange for teaching us all how to ride. I broached the subject with the kids; their little eyes opened wide with enthusiasm. After growing up with a small suburban backyard, the prospect of riding horses around the grounds inspired them to break into an excitable dance.

I took that as a 'yes'.

Huîtres
D'Isigny s/mer
4€/ 13 à
Dou

The Norman table

Moving to Bosgouet opened up a whole new gastronomic experience for our family. We had an enviable opportunity to sample the best the region had to offer. The people of Normandy are legendary for their marvellous hospitality, which almost always revolves around the table. I've always felt a great thrill in being a hostess; I think that the ritual of eating together inextricably binds friends and family. The Normans' penchant for entertaining strengthens the affinity I feel I have with them.

In Normandy the business of eating is taken extremely seriously and the topic of food is accorded the utmost respect, as you might expect from a people who have been producing Camembert since the seventeenth century. The perfect accompaniment to a plate of *fromages* is given grave consideration; that fresh, hand-picked fig does not appear there by accident. The elements remain the same whether one is purchasing veggies on a Saturday morning at the bustling organic market at place Sainte Catherine in the fishing port of Honfleur, or enjoying a *menu dégustation* at a Michelin-starred restaurant. Cuisine in Normandy is founded on the principle of always using the freshest seasonal ingredients. Perhaps the apples piled up in carts at every farmers market in Normandy are destined for a fluffy apple tart, served with fresh cream. Or perhaps they will be distilled into Calvados, a wicked and warming brandy used to clear the palate between courses. Firm favourites in the kitchens of Normandy include crème fraîche and cheeses such as Camembert, Livarot and Pont-l'Évêque. The Normans will always cook with the best butter available, used in liberal amounts. Normandy is not a place you come to diet.

Fruit and vegetable market near
la Cathédrale Sainte-Catherine, Honfleur.

Locals who run food stores or market stalls will often do a little something extra when you purchase food. Unfailingly your requests will be greeted with an obliging '*Mais oui*' (but yes). Six-dozen oysters from the Vieux-Marché in Rouen opened and arranged on an iced platter ready for serving? '*Mais oui, Madame Webster.*'

One of my favourite butchers has his *boucherie* in the nearby village of Bourgtheroulde. One day Monsieur prepared incredibly tender escalopes of milk-fed veal while I waited, at every stage showing me his handiwork and asking for my approval with the customary '*Ça va?*' Madame, *la bouchère*, then appeared from a room at the back of the shop, as if sensing that the strange Australian was here again needing help with the pieces of veal her husband was so fastidiously preparing. Madame suggested that I season the escalopes with salt and pepper, flour them and then sauté them in a heavy skillet with some butter. To make the sauce, she patiently instructed, I must sauté shallots, add a little brown stock, and then deglaze the pan with a good Riesling.

'Make sure to reduce the liquid and then add some crème fraîche and horseradish,' she cautioned, as if a mistake would lead to a monumental catastrophe.

I should then spoon the sauce over the veal and serve it with julienne vegetables and freshly made noodles. As she gave me these final directives, Madame sighed with delight, as if she had just eaten the meal herself instead of merely instructing me on it.

I followed Madame's instructions to the letter and her recipe has since become a family favourite. When I returned to the *boucherie* the next day to thank her for her expert advice Madame graciously offered to assist me with other recipes. She encouraged me to experiment with different cuts of meat.

A fishmonger prepares les coquilles at the market in Dieppe.

Duck is extremely popular in Normandy. Madame walked me through the traditional preparation of cooking duck breast by poaching it in duck fat. This method makes the meat extremely tender. Madame's favourite way of serving the breast is to slice it thinly and serve it on top of a simple salad of rocket, endive, home-grown tomatoes and walnuts pan-fried in the rendered duck fat. Delicious!

The Normans love their long Sunday lunches and this ritual was fully embraced at Château de Bosgouet. It became an important event in our calendar. In Bourg-Achard, a village only a kilometre down the road, all the food shops are open every Sunday morning especially so that people can procure provisions for their midday feast. The door to Monsieur Alix's main street *boucherie* opens around 8.30 a.m. Those keen to purchase a cut of his prize-winning beef or veal without having to line up for a hundred metres down the street best get in early. Eager cooks or their assistants wait patiently to purchase the centrepiece of their Sunday lunch. No one is ever grouchy at the slow progress of the line – the result is worth the wait. This is normally where my Sunday morning began. Often I wouldn't know in advance what I'd be cooking, instead I'd diligently watch each customer and listen carefully to the instructions the butcher gave them. Or, as so often happens in these situations, one of the customers would spontaneously volunteer a favourite recipe.

One particular Sunday morning an elderly lady a dozen places down the queue interrupted my conversation with Monsieur Alix to put forward her own recipe for pork belly, defending her particular recipe and technique with the conviction of a Michelin-star chef. *That's the glory of France*, I thought

as I left the shop with the recipe still buzzing around in my head. I was inspired by everyone's willingness to share their ideas, trusted techniques and even their secret ingredients. Perhaps they thought I needed all the help I could get. After all, not being French I obviously lacked the refined palate that only those who have been schooled in the ways of the gourmet since infancy can boast.

Sometimes simply buying the ingredients for Sunday lunch took up all morning. Once I had visited *la boucherie*, the next stop was *la cour de halle* where a variety of beautifully arranged fresh seasonal fruit and vegetables, herbs and raw-milk Norman cheeses can be purchased. Here, those who do not have a cellar can also find a good selection of white and red wines, Champagnes and dessert wines. Normandy excels at cider rather than wine production, so most of these bottles will come from elsewhere in France. Next, as no French meal would be complete without freshly baked bread, it would be off to the *boulangerie* for some crusty baguettes.

I learnt a sober lesson about bread very early on in our stay when my friend and language tutor, Annik, brought her father to Bosgouet for a meal. My French friend came to me just as I was serving the meal, looking alarmed.

'Jane, do you have bread?' she whispered. 'My father will not eat unless he has bread at the table.' I chuckled and rolled my eyes, but Annik went on, deadpan. 'Really. He will not eat unless there is bread.'

Poor Annik. I thought she might pop a vein in her brow, the worry being just too great. I did, of course, have bread, and both father and daughter looked much more at ease after I'd placed the bread basket in front of them. Such is the importance of the ostensibly humble loaf.

Lastly on a Sunday morning I would pick up a box of *petits fours*, unable to resist the strawberry tarts, chocolate éclairs, cream puffs and *tartlettes au*

citron. I always made a dessert, too, but often we finished our Sunday meal with these tiny, tasty mouthfuls, served with our coffee and chocolates.

Millie and Maddie were wonderful helpers in the château's kitchen. Indeed, they were becoming accomplished cooks in their own right. Little Alex was also an eager participant in preparing Sunday lunch, her favourite activity being to peel the veggies. An incredible feeling comes over me when my family gathers together to cook. I love the fact that I am able to pass on this appreciation of 'the table' to my children. At Bosgouet our conversations wound through many topics, but often these discussions over the preparation of Sunday lunch were a way of making sense of our French experience, and of the central role that food was playing in our new lives.

In a world where people are increasingly eating on the run – standing at the bench, or even in the car – I am so grateful for the pause meal times give our family. I like to think of these times as periods of gentle instruction in the arts of manners and conversation, in the art of being social. I think we can all learn something from the French insistence that food and the rituals of eating do – and must – enrich our lives.

Frites at Le Neubourg.

Monsieur, the fromage-wrangler, doles out crème fraîche for us to take home.

A French Easter

France, with its deep Catholic roots, really goes to town with its Easter celebrations. Village shops are elaborately decorated with Easter motifs — rabbits, chicken, fish and bells — and draped in brightly coloured streamers. There is a national three-day holiday, so everyone can participate in the festivities.

French children follow the Easter tradition of Poisson d'Avril *(April fish)*. On 1 April French children play an April Fools-type trick. A paper fish is stuck to the back of as many unwitting adults as possible — the kids then run away with cries of 'Poisson d'Avril!' This tradition dates back several centuries. It is said to have evolved from a different sort of trick where villagers would send an unsuspecting person to the market to buy freshwater fish when it was not in season.

Another important tradition is the cloche volante *(flying bell)*. From the day before Good Friday until Easter morning all bells are silenced. French Catholics tell their children that the bells have flown to the Vatican, taking with them the grief felt by all those who mourn the crucifixion of Jesus. On Sunday morning the bells ring out joyously in celebration of the resurrection — the flying bells have returned from Rome, and they have brought chocolate eggs with them. Kids then take part in an Easter hunt; les oeufs de Pâques *are normally hidden in nests or in the garden.*

After the eggs have been found, the family might take part in a few customary Easter games. A favourite is a contest where raw eggs are rolled down a slope — symbolising the boulder that was rolled away from Jesus' tomb. The owner of the surviving egg is crowned the victor. In another game kids throw a raw egg up into the air; the first to drop it loses and must give away one of their chocolate eggs as a penalty.

A typical Easter Sunday dinner might last as long as five or six hours and the family will feast on spring lamb or goat served with fresh, new-season vegetables, like artichokes and asparagus.

The potager at Bosgouet

Outside the château *le printemps* was in full swing. The countryside was a vast patchwork: perfect squares of flaxseed yellow against those of vivid green. In a nearby field baby lambs kept close to their mother as they sheltered from the hot midday sun under brilliant umbrellas of blossom. Everything felt bright and auspicious and I was full of anticipation for the possibilities and new experiences that spring would bring with it. Pete and I had been planning the restoration of the parkland at the château. When we arrived at Bosgouet there were no gardens as such, just lawn, trees and a few shrubs, but the place was a right mess – everything was overgrown, especially the weeds, and debris from the trees lay everywhere. I winced at the thought of more cleaning; it felt like we'd only just finished getting the house in order. It was a smaller project that filled me with a sense of purpose and excitement: planting a potager in the ancient walled garden on the right-hand side of the château. Even though I'm an amateur gardener – all enthusiasm, little skill – I felt that this was the perfect opportunity to improve my green thumb.

The term potager comes from *potage*, French for soup, as these gardens were historically used by French peasants to grow soup vegetables. The tradition evolved and 'potager' became a general term for a kitchen garden where vegetables, fruit, flowers and herbs are cultivated for the consumption of the household. As well as following certain horticultural principles to help these different kinds of produce grow side by side, potagers traditionally have a formal geometric design, most commonly square or rectangular garden beds. These are often sheltered by high brick walls to temper seasonal extremes.

The most famous example is Le Potager du Roi in Versailles, commissioned in 1678 by the 'Sun King', Louis XIV. King Louis employed a lawyer-turned-landscape gardener by the name of Jean-Baptiste de la Quintinye to convert soggy marshland into a splendid garden large enough to help feed the palace's population of 3000 people. King Louis himself had a reputation for being a terrible glutton. He was infamous for the 'prodigious amount' of salad he ate each year. At Bosgouet we eat a fair amount of salad ourselves, so our sympathies lie with poor Louis. Louis' potager covered over 20 acres of land and included twenty-nine elaborate walled garden 'rooms'. Now only eleven garden beds exist, but over 5000 fruit trees are still cultivated and they produce over 4 tonnes of fruit a year. De la Quintinye established fruit and vegetable pruning systems that are still employed by modern gardeners.

At Bosgouet we had a plan to become as self-sufficient as possible, and I was keen to fill our own acre-wide potager with my favourite fruit, vegetables, flowers and herbs. Our aim was to design and plant a garden where aesthetics and practicality met – to create an edible garden that was also beautiful to look at. Our potager would have to supply enough produce for my family during our stay, and the château's caretakers and gardeners, who were here all year round. In addition, I'd need supplies each summer for The French Table. We had expected to begin working on the potager in early spring, but the year before had seen a particularly long and arduous winter. Seeds will not come up if they are sown before the soil is warm. So we had to put our planting on hold for longer than we'd intended. We used this time to refine our design.

In Normandy gardens are considered an art form and have been part of the region's culture for centuries. There were many spectacular gardens that we had to visit in the name of research, including Monet's garden at Giverny and the potager at Château Beaumensil. Pete and I took many field trips to look at these gardens for inspiration in design, planting and construction.

Our sixteenth-century stables were untouched by the fire that destroyed the original château.

Jordy, one of Monsieur
Christophe's horses.

We spoke to many skilful gardeners for advice on considerations such as the best ways to lay pathways and edgings, build raised beds, organise compost bins, and erect espalier frames and plant supports. We found all to be generous in sharing their knowledge, but the sheer amount of information about the potagers was close to being overwhelming. Take, for instance, the litany of horticultural edicts that one must follow: rotate crops, compost, companion plant, and use organic gardening methods . . . I struggled to keep all of this in my non-gardener's head! It would have been foolish to rush things. That spring we made a decent start on the potager, but we knew that it would be an ongoing project, one that would extend long after our first sojourn in Normandy had ended.

The potager we laid the foundations for followed a formal design, with a central axis and the rest of the garden divided into squares. The borders will be defined by box hedging (once it grows!) and the pathways will be made from crushed rock.

Many mornings as I lay in bed, the sun streaming through the French windows, I daydreamed of July or August when the first crops in other people's potagers would be ready for eating – French beans, salad greens and leeks, followed by celery, cabbages and beetroots. I was impatient and could not possibly wait for our formal potager to mature, so I planted a small one of my own outside the kitchen door.

My little garden, which is both conveniently placed and, according to Pete, unruly, is filled with sage, rosemary, thyme, basil, tarragon, a small bay tree, parsley and chives. I even have enough room to grow some rocket and a tangle of cherry tomatoes.

My garden has a cottage feel about it and often gets overgrown, but it produces enough herbs for us throughout the summer months. I fight for my garden to stay put by promising to try harder to keep it looking neat. Gardening satisfies something in me, even if I'm guided only by guesswork and blind enthusiasm. I love the tranquillity I feel from bringing together a formal, well-planned garden, but there's something about it that can't quite match the exuberance of planting spontaneously.

Spring
recipes

Cheese Sables

These delicate little appetisers are given a hint of spice by the cayenne pepper and are delicious served with a glass or two of sparkling white wine. Makes about 28.

INGREDIENTS

200 g plain (all-purpose) flour
200 g grated cheese (either all
cheddar or half cheddar and
half Parmesan)
200 g unsalted butter
large pinch of salt
¼ teaspoon cayenne pepper
squeeze of lemon juice

METHOD

Place all ingredients into a food processor and pulse together to form a dough. Divide dough in half, then roll into 2 long sausage shapes. Wrap in plastic film and chill in the refrigerator for 1 hour.

Preheat oven to 200°C (400°F).

On a lightly floured surface, cut dough into 2 cm-thick rounds. Place on a baking tray lined with baking paper. Bake for 15 minutes. Cool on a wire rack.

Cheese sables will keep for up to 1 week in an airtight container.

Normandy Bisque

This soup has a rich, creamy flavour and is traditionally served as an entrée in a deep two-handled cup. Serves 6.

INGREDIENTS

1 tablespoon olive oil
700 g cooked medium prawns, peeled, with heads and shells reserved
2 onions, finely chopped
1 carrot, sliced
2 stalks celery, sliced
1 small red chilli, seeds removed, finely sliced
¼ cup lemon juice
1 tablespoon tomato purée
1 bouquet garni (made up of 1 bay leaf, a sprig of flat-leaf parsley and a sprig of thyme)
80 g butter
¼ cup plain (all-purpose) flour
¼ cup Calvados (or brandy)
sea salt and freshly ground black pepper
¾ cup pouring cream

METHOD

Heat oil in a large, heavy-based saucepan and add the prawn heads and shells, then cook over high heat, stirring all the time until they start to colour. Reduce heat to low, then add onions, carrot, celery and chilli and cook gently for 6–8 minutes or until vegetables start to soften.

Add 2 litres water, 2 tablespoons of the lemon juice, tomato purée and bouquet garni. Bring to the boil and simmer over low heat for 30 minutes. Strain stock into a large bowl through a muslin-lined sieve. Meanwhile, melt butter into a large heavy-based saucepan. Stir in flour and cook until golden. Add brandy and pour in half of the prawn stock; whisk continuously until smooth. Slowly add remaining stock. Season to taste.

Strain soup into a clean saucepan. Add cream and remaining lemon juice and season to taste again. Stir in the reserved prawns and cook over medium heat for 1–2 minutes or until prawns are heated through.

Serve at once.

Lou's Potato and Spinach Soup

My dear friend Lou came to visit Bosgouet early in our adventure. Each day we would shop at the market and then cook together in the basement kitchen. This is a delicious soup that Lou came up with one spring Sunday. Serves 6.

INGREDIENTS

60 g butter
3 onions, roughly chopped
3 stalks celery, roughly chopped
5 large potatoes, roughly chopped
1 litre chicken stock
1 kg spinach leaves
½ cup clotted cream
sea salt and freshly ground
    black pepper
freshly grated Parmesan and
    baguette, to serve

METHOD

Melt the butter and sauté onions and celery in a cast-iron casserole over low heat for 8–10 minutes or until just soft but not browned. Add potatoes and stock. Bring to the boil over high heat, then reduce heat to low and simmer for 20 minutes or until tender. Purée with a hand-held blender, then return to heat and add spinach a handful at a time, stirring until wilted. Season to taste.

Serve topped with a sprinkle of freshly grated Parmesan and crusty fresh baguette to the side.

Whole Atlantic Salmon with Dill Dressing

Poaching salmon keeps the flesh wonderfully moist and full of flavour. This recipe was a real favourite with our neighbours Amy and Todd. While the fish was cooling we'd all duck outside for a game or two of *pétanque*.
Serves 8–10.

INGREDIENTS

1 x 2.5 kg Atlantic salmon (ask your fishmonger to remove head, clean and scale)
2 cups white wine
1 large lemon, sliced
¼ teaspoon black peppercorns

Dill Dressing
1 cup yoghurt
½ cup chopped dill
sea salt and freshly ground black pepper
sliced cucumber and lemon (optional), to serve

METHOD

Place salmon in a fish poacher with white wine, 1 litre water, slices of lemon and peppercorns, then bring to the boil, reduce heat to low and poach gently for 10 minutes. Remove from heat and leave salmon in poacher for 1–2 hours to cool completely; the fish will continue to cook.

Meanwhile, for the dill dressing, mix the yoghurt with dill and season to taste.

Carefully remove salmon from poacher and place on a platter, then use a small sharp knife to remove the skin from the side facing upwards. Decorate if you wish with thinly sliced cucumber and lemon. Serve with the dill dressing passed separately.

Milk-fed Veal with Vermouth and Tarragon

Don't be fooled by this recipe's simplicity; it's a knockout. The subtle flavour of the pale-coloured, tender escalopes is wonderfully contrasted with the dry Vermouth. Serves 6.

INGREDIENTS

60 g butter
6 x 150 g milk-fed veal escalopes
   (sold as veal schnitzel
   or medallions)
1 clove garlic, finely chopped
½–1 tablespoon lemon juice
½ cup dry Vermouth
2 tablespoons French tarragon or
   finely chopped flat-leaf parsley,
   to serve

METHOD

Melt butter in a frying pan over high heat, then sauté veal for 3 minutes on each side. Add garlic and lemon juice, then pour in Vermouth and bring to the boil. Reduce heat to low and cook for 10 minutes. Just before serving, sprinkle with chopped tarragon and parsley.

Salad of Beetroot, Pink Grapefruit, Goat's Cheese and Mint

This salad makes a tasty and spectacular-looking side dish; it's perfect with chicken or fish. Serves 6–8.

INGREDIENTS

4 small beetroot
olive oil, for cooking
2 pink grapefruit, peeled and cut
   into small bite-sized pieces
125 g goat's cheese
chopped mint, to serve
1 x quantity Bosgouet Vinaigrette
   (see page 110)

METHOD

Preheat oven to 180°C (350°F).

Place beetroot on a baking tray, drizzle with olive oil and roast for 30 minutes or until tender when pierced with a skewer. Leave beetroot to cool, then peel and cut into bite-sized chunks.

Combine beetroot, grapefruit and goat's cheese on a large platter and scatter with freshly chopped mint. Serve drizzled with Bosgouet Vinaigrette.

Strawberry Tartlets

The whole family really fell for these little delights while we were in Normandy. They are gorgeous to look at and devilishly difficult to resist. Makes 32.

INGREDIENTS

icing sugar, for dusting

Shortcrust Pastry
125 g plain (all-purpose) flour
pinch of salt
55 g butter, chopped
30–45 ml cold water

Apricot Glaze
1¼ cups apricot jam
2 tablespoons Calvados or rum

Strawberry Filling
750 g ripe strawberries, washed, hulled and patted dry with kitchen paper
½ cup white sugar
2–3 tablespoons cornflour
¼ cup cold water
2 tablespoons lime juice

METHOD

For shortcrust pastry, sift flour and salt into a large bowl. With your fingertips, rub butter into the flour until the mixture looks like coarse breadcrumbs. It's important to use cold butter; if the butter melts, the pastry will become tough and chewy. Stir in a little of the cold water, but only use enough to bind the mix: too much will make for a sticky mess. Wrap the dough in plastic wrap and chill in the refrigerator for 15 minutes.

Preheat oven to 180°C (350°F). Roll pastry out on a lightly floured bench to a 3 mm thickness. Cut out circles to fit your tartlet pans. Fit circles into lightly greased pans. Blind bake using rice or pastry weights for 15 minutes or until golden.

Meanwhile, for apricot glaze, bring jam and Calvados to the boil in a small saucepan over medium heat, stirring often. Cook, stirring continuously, for 2–3 minutes or until jam is very sticky. Strain through a sieve into a bowl, pressing down on solids; keep warm. $\longrightarrow$

Remove tart shells from oven and brush insides
with hot apricot glaze, then leave to cool.

For the strawberry filling, cut half of the
strawberries in halves or quarters, then scatter over
the pastry bases. Roughly mash the remaining
strawberries, then mix through sugar and pop
them into a saucepan. Slowly bring to a simmer
over low heat, stirring frequently. Cook for
2–3 minutes or until strawberries collapse.

Meanwhile, mix 2–3 tablespoons of cornflour with
the cold water and add lime juice. Pour this paste
into the strawberry mixture and keep stirring until
it thickens. Spoon strawberry purée evenly over
strawberries in pastry cases.

Refrigerate for 1–2 hours, then dust with icing
sugar before serving.

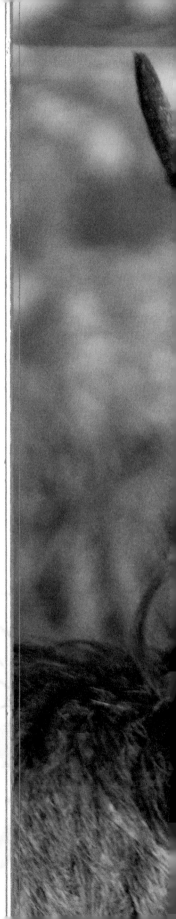

Honey and Lavender Madeleine Cakes

Madeleine cakes will forever be associated with Marcel Proust's masterpiece *Rememberance of Things Past*. A bite into one of these buttery little cakes releases a flood of childhood memories for Proust's protagonist. You, too, will always remember your first taste. Makes 18.

INGREDIENTS

100 g butter, plus extra,
  for greasing
2 tablespoons honey
3 eggs
⅓ cup caster (superfine) sugar
1 tablespoon soft brown sugar
½ teaspoon vanilla extract
100 g self-raising (self-rising) flour
2 organic or unsprayed lavender
  sprigs, finely chopped
plain (all-purpose) flour, for dusting
icing sugar, for dusting

METHOD

Melt butter and honey in a small saucepan over low heat and put in a medium-sized bowl to cool. Once cool, add eggs, one at a time, then add both sugars and vanilla, and sift in flour. Stir lavender flowers into the mixture. Preheat the oven to 180°C (350°F).

Prepare a madeleine cake pan by brushing with melted butter and dusting with flour. Spoon 1 tablespoon of batter into each madeleine mould, then bake for 10 minutes. Cool in the madeleine pan for 5 minutes before turning out onto wire racks to cool. Dust cooled madeleines with icing sugar before serving.

Raspberry Almond Clafoutis

Clafoutis is a favourite French pudding-style dessert. It is typically made with cherries, but I think raspberries give this recipe a lovely piquancy. Serves 6.

INGREDIENTS

½ cup ground almonds
1 cup milk
butter, for greasing
½ cup caster (superfine) sugar
2 cups raspberries
3 large eggs, at room temperature
¼ teaspoon almond extract
pinch of salt
⅓ cup plain (all-purpose) flour
icing sugar, for dusting

METHOD

In a small saucepan, bring ground almonds and milk to a simmer over low heat. Remove from heat. Leave almond milk to intensify in flavour for 1 hour, then pour through a sieve, discarding any solids.

Preheat oven to 180°C (350°F).

Butter a 25 cm pie dish. Sprinkle the dish with 1 tablespoon of the sugar. Scatter raspberries evenly over the bottom of the dish.

Beat eggs, almond extract, salt and remaining sugar in a bowl until well blended. Add almond milk and continue to beat. Sift flour into egg mixture and beat until smooth. Pour mixture over raspberries.

Bake for 35–40 minutes or until clafoutis is set. Cool completely.

Lightly dust clafoutis with icing sugar before serving.

Bosgouet Vinaigrette

This is a staple in the Bosgouet larder. Fresh garden greens thrown together with some herbs and a splash of vinaigrette ensures a healthy and delicious side dish for any meal. Makes about 1 cup.

INGREDIENTS

¼ cup white-wine vinegar
2 golden shallots, finely chopped
½ teaspoon sea salt
1 teaspoon Dijon mustard
freshly ground black pepper
¾ cup extra virgin olive oil

METHOD

Place all ingredients into a clean jar and shake until they have emulsified.

Store in a cool place for up to 1 month.

Farm-fresh Yoghurt

Making fresh yoghurt is such a simple and satisfying job. The yoghurt will keep stored in the refrigerator for up to 1 week. Makes 1 litre.

INGREDIENTS

1 litre full-cream milk
1 tablespoon natural yoghurt

METHOD

Heat milk in a heavy-based saucepan over low heat until milk is just about to boil.

Mix in natural yoghurt, using a whisk to combine. Pour mixture into 4 x 250 ml sterilised jam jars and leave to cool at room temperature for 6–8 hours, until the yoghurt is set.

Sous le tilleul
(under the linden tree)

Spring passed too quickly, and with it came the end of the French school year and the start of the long summer vacation. Pete and I turned our attention to the kids, working out how to keep them amused until school resumed in September. We had organised a number of short trips to beaches in the south of France, near Biarritz, and further down over the Spanish border to San Sebastian. We were also expecting quite a few house guests during the summer months. I was sure that the lively parade of family and friends would keep us all entertained.

In high summer we began, almost invariably, to take our meals out-side, sitting under the shade of an ancient linden tree; its massive branches giving us protection from the fierce July sun. The weather was so glorious that I could barely face being stuck indoors, so with a bit of clever rearrang-ing I relocated some of my daily activities outside, such as preparing and cooking most of our meals. I decided that those chores that couldn't be done outdoors probably weren't worth doing anyway.

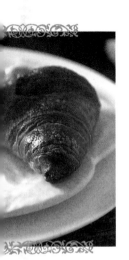

Our summer pattern was a simple one. Each morning I would take out all the breakfast comestibles to a large stone table that had travelled with us from Australia. In our garden in Melbourne the table for twelve always seemed enormous, but here it was dwarfed by the sheer magnitude of the park and house. Typically, everyone who happened to be staying at the château would eventually wake up and lazily make their way outside to the table, where we would all sit and read the papers, chat, paint, write and eat well into the morning.

Breakfast was usually a combination of fresh fruit, yoghurt and bircher muesli as well as fresh *pâtisseries* from the local *boulangerie*. It would be wrong not to have croissants, *pain au chocolat*, brioche and homemade jams when breakfasting in France. The children retained their firm favourites from home; they loved it when I made them pancakes or raspberry muffins.

In these morning assemblies significant energy was devoted to the topic of food. We would discuss the day's menu, whether we would prepare the meals inside in the basement kitchen or outside on the barbecue (it was almost always the latter), which markets were best for a certain type of produce, and who was to be delegated the solemn responsibility of buying the provisions. Happily, I almost always got the job of visiting the markets. I love to choose the food I am going to cook with and I could never pass up an opportunity to

Œufs +73 gr.
à
Pièce : 0,25 EUROS
Boîte vide : 0,20 EUROS

speak with the farmers themselves about their produce, not to mention their recipe ideas.

Those long summer days were generally unstructured, but we did keep a strict appointment for aperitif hour, which kicked off at 6 p.m. Not a day went by that the entire household didn't get together for a drink and a nibble of something delicious to sustain us until dinnertime. A rustic old table from one of the stables was salvaged from years of lying idle, dusted off and promoted to Aperitif Table. We set this table with pretty tea towels for tablecloths, glasses and an ample amount of ice. Little bowls of pistachios and olives sat alongside blinis, smoked salmon or chicken wings. The drink choice was updated nightly – Kir Royale, vodka, tonic and lime, or the anise-flavoured Pastis. There was always homemade lemon cordial on hand for the kids and our teetotalling friends. We invented a few memorable cocktails that summer, and their effects will live on in the annals of our private history. One such cocktail is the Jonquay, a speciality of our neighbours Amy and Todd who own nearby Château Jonquay. It's a lethal mixture of lemon juice, Calvados and Cointreau. Delicious, but oh so dangerous!

We shared aperitif hour with many of our new friends. What better way to get to know people than over a flute of French bubbles and a tray of delicious morsels? Most of these evenings we had at least a dozen adults and another dozen children to feed at dinnertime. If we were feeling formal, we would drag another table outside so that everyone could eat together, but most often night picnics sufficed and we would just throw rugs on the lawn.

A typical meal would consist of two or three appetisers to go with an aperitif – say cheese sables and bruschetta topped with tomatoes and basil from the garden, crunchy croutons (made from yesterday's baguettes) and crumbled goat's cheese. The entrée might be a huge pot of mussels from the

Aperitifs under our favourite linden tree.

Normandy coast cooked in white wine, herbs, ginger, shallots, garlic and a hint of chilli. I always served this with crusty fresh baguettes to sop up the juices. For the next course we might have a leg of Normandy lamb slow-roasted on the barbecue. The main course would be served with salads and tiny *pommes charlotte* cooked in rich duck fat.

After dinner, the kids would bring out boardgames and conduct fiercely competitive rounds of Monopoly or Scrabble, while the adults would either cheer from the sidelines or join in a game or two themselves. Other favourite after-dinner activities were concerts or plays produced, directed and performed by the children. The main steps of Bosgouet create the perfect stage, with the audience sitting happily on the grass below, cheering on the performers. Something about Bosgouet brings out people's inner thespians and divas, so we were occasionally treated to a performance by one of our adult guests. Even I've been known to do an impromptu version of '*Je Ne Regrette Rien*'.

Once a week or so, part of our coterie – an amateur astronomy club – would arrive in convoy at Bosgouet and set up their huge telescopes. The park would be dotted with folding chairs and picnic rugs. We'd take turns looking through the lenses at the night-time spectacle. The sky was blissfully unclouded by skyscrapers, smog or city lights. Being introduced to various constellations and watching out for comets and asteroids requires sustenance, so I'd make pots of coffee and tea and hand around slices of cake or plates of biscuits. There were many summer nights that I went to bed and dreamt of galaxies and star formations.

Pétanque

The game of pétanque, *otherwise known as* boules, *is a sport close to the hearts of many French citizens. Although it bears some similarity to British lawn bowls or Italian* bocce, *the French version is traditionally played with metallic balls on a dirt surface beneath plane trees.*

The object of the game is to throw the ball along the ground, usually with an arched back-spin, so that it lands closer to the cochonnet *(the small object ball) than those of your opponents. You can also strike the object ball and drive it toward your other balls and away from your opponents'.*

The local boulodrome *is a social focal point in France. Most villages have a place specially designated in the village square where people can be seen playing every day, particularly in the summer months. At Bosgouet we like to play before dinner, with a glass of Pastis always at hand.*

Beachside at Deauville and Étretat.

During the summer months, we spent most Tuesdays and Fridays in Deauville for the seaside town's legendary market days, when local farmers gather to sell their produce. Deauville is often referred to as 'the most elegant lady in Normandy'. This genteel village is also cheekily known as the twenty-first arrondissement of Paris as it is over-run by Parisians each weekend. Our band of intrepid travellers usually consisted of Pete and me, our four adventurers and a handful of our visitors who would have heard me rhapsodise about Deauville. After tumbling out of the cars, the others would head straight to the beach to try to beat the hot weather, while I would set a course for the marketplace in the heart of the town.

Since one needs to be alert during these outings, I would usually start with *un café* at a smart nearby brasserie. I always find it best to head to the markets with an open mind. I can spend hours roaming the stalls keeping my eye out for what looks tastiest, has the best colour and, of course, what is in season. At Deauville my favourite summer purchase was courgettes. I love to peel them lengthwise and throw them in a pan with a knob of good-quality butter and some rose-pink garlic, sautéing the ribbons just long enough to warm them through. The tomatoes at that time of year were irresistible, too, and teaming them with herbs and salad vegetables was enough to lift any meal.

I would purchase peaches and punnets of strawberries, knowing that it was unlikely that these items would last long enough to make their way back to Bosgouet. Seafood is a speciality at Deauville, so I'd pick up succulent fillets of sardines, Saint Pierre (John Dory) or mussels. With the mid-summer days being so blazing hot, I quickly got into the habit of keeping an old blue Esky in the back of the car.

Once I had picked up enough ingredients for dinner, I'd turn my attention to the more pressing matter of what to feed the beach-goers. I'd fill my wicker

basket with fresh baguettes, cheese, plump tomatoes, crispy green lettuce and hot rotisserie chickens and wander over to the beach to find the rest of the party. I did this often enough to be a dab hand at the impromptu lunch, so the basket was always equipped with a small cutting board and knife as well as a large stock of paper napkins. I also packed cutlery in case I was unable to resist one of the market stalls' huge pots of paella or the *pommes de terre* (potatoes) cooked in the juices and fat of the rotisserie chickens. There were days when temptation got the better of me and I couldn't say no to this 'fast market food'.

Deauville is the perfect spot for a beach picnic without the agony of sandy sandwiches. It has manicured gardens that run the entire stretch of the fore-shore, as well as a wonderful wooden esplanade (*les planches*). After lunch we would take the children for a stroll along *les planches*, and perhaps buy them an ice-cream at one of the nearby stalls. Customarily, the adults would then watch the children play on the beach from the vantage point of a beachfront restaurant, while enjoying a coffee, or perhaps something stronger.

Although Deauville was a favourite spot for beach picnics and market days, we found lots of other spots nearby that gave us equal pleasure. On occasions when we were feeling adventurous, we ventured further afield to other Norman seaside resorts: Etretat, Veules-les-Roses, Paris-Plage and Fécamp.

And after a long day at the seaside, there was nothing better than returning to Bosgouet to sit under the shade of our linden tree to feast on fresh snapper served with *frites*, followed by a game of *pétanque* on the lawn.

Linden tisane

There are two varieties of the linden tree, Tilia platyphyllos *and* Tilia cordata, *called the summer and winter linden. They look pretty much alike, but* Tilia platyphyllos *flowers some two weeks earlier than* Tilia cordata. *The linden tree is considered sacred, and you can often find very old examples – up to 1000 years old – at the centre of villages or in front of churches. Our linden tree at Bosgouet is well over 300 years old.*

When I first came to Bosgouet, I smelt the rich, honey-like fragrance of our linden tree long before I saw it. We turned a corner in the driveway and the tree came into view: small green-and-yellow flowers dangled from oblong, wing-like bracts. My brother-in-law, Theo, told me how the French made tea from the flowers or leaves of the linden tree.

Linden tea has a delicious taste; it is one of the French's favourite tisanes. It is warming and stimulating, and makes an excellent remedy for colds and fever. There is a lot of mucilage in linden flowers. This gives them a soothing, healing quality when the infusion comes into contact with the membranes of the digestive system. This demulcent action, combined with the relaxing factor, has also led to the use of the tea for indigestion. It is easy to make, too. You can obtain the dried flowers from health-food stores and they are even available in tea bags.

Use a heaped teaspoonful (2–4 g) of the crushed flowers per cup of boiling water. As with all herbal teas, it is important not to allow the steam to escape. This is crucial when using linden flowers because the relaxing properties depend on the volatile oils, which can easily evaporate and be lost in the steam. That's why you should carefully cover the teapot or make linden tea in a jar with a screw-top lid. If you are in a restaurant, you can place your saucer over the cup containing the tea bag while the flowers are steeping. They should be steeped for about 10 minutes.

Drink three cups each day. A typical course of treatment lasts around three months.

Fireworks and bonfires

The festivities that commemorate the storming of the Bastille on la Fête Nationale (Bastille Day) are not to be missed. We were expecting our first 14 July in Bosgouet to be quite an understated affair. After all, the village has a tiny population. We wandered into the village anticipating only a drowsy toast or two or maybe a half-hearted cry of '*Vive la France*'. Instead, the streets were decked with flags and streamers, a band was playing in the square and every person in the village was out celebrating. In Bosgouet the Bastille celebrations last for three days, commencing with a mass in the village church that sits on the edge of Château de Bosgouet, and culminating in a fireworks display.

The village has always used the château's park for the fireworks display and we were keen to continue this tradition. Faithless folk that we were we expected the fireworks to be a bit of a flop, the equivalent of an Australian backyard cracker night. We had built up an enormous bonfire, which we thought would liven things up if the fireworks fizzled out. In the end the fireworks needed no such help; they were spectacular. The night sky was lit up with bursts of colour.

Catholicism is deeply ingrained in the culture of French rural villages, and religious feast days and national holidays still bring people out in all their finery, ready to indulge in food, wine and socialising – once mass has been said, of course. Most of these holiday occasions are taken extremely seriously by every French man, woman and child. Fireworks and bonfires have long been used as a symbol of celebration in France and are an integral part of many French customs. They are an expression of rejoicing and are used to mark great victories.

We took on this tradition with great gusto. During the rest of the summer we held many bonfire nights to celebrate private occasions, such as a birthday. Just the merest whisper of the word 'bonfire' at Château de Bosgouet and the whole house was abuzz with excitement. The children would eagerly jump on the back of the tractor, ready to gather wood with Pete by clearing the bracken from the floor of the surrounding forests. In the early days at Bosgouet bonfire night had the added benefit of aiding the cleaning up of the grounds. The various wood scraps that been left by previous owners – broken chairs and tables and a perplexing number of old desks – made for excellent firewood.

On these nights our neighbours and everyone staying at Bosgouet would join us for aperitifs and a barbecue dinner before the ritual of lighting the bonfire. There would be a countdown to the first lick of flame and then the festivities would begin: dancing and singing from adults and children alike. We'd toast marshmallows and drink coffee or hot chocolate around the fire until well after midnight.

The flames of the bonfire brought together a group of people who otherwise would never have met. The guests who came to visit us from all over the world mixed with our local French friends. Any timid glances or awkward smiles soon gave way to breezy conversation, laughter and affectionate back-slaps. It made me think that it isn't just the history or architecture that is Château de Bosgouet's soul, but the friendships and ties forged by firelight.

Fromage et liqueur

I have often heard that to truly understand a place you must know its cuisine. It has been a great pleasure to become acquainted with Normandy; I now consider us to be firm friends. I have spent a lot of time in the Seine-Maritime region methodically trying out various eateries, noting the outstanding examples. Some of the most exceptional food I have tasted has not necessarily been the most elaborately constructed fare. In fact, quite the contrary is true. The Normans are cussedly resistant to the tortured and overworked products of *nouvelle cuisine*. This is a matter of regional pride, of course, but the Normans have been doing food and drink so well for so long, why on earth would they try to keep up with fleeting fashions?

On the weekend our family would often have lunch in one of half a dozen restaurants that line the banks of the Seine in the village of La Bouille, downstream from Rouen. La Bouille is only 3 kilometres from Bosgouet and was a favourite haunt of ours. One of the best cheese trolleys we have found in Normandy is at the Saint Pierre restaurant in La Bouille. The trolley has over thirty different cheeses, all locally produced, including Camembert, Livarot, Pont-l'Évêque and Neufchâtel. The restaurant sits right on the bank of the Seine, and as the diners savour the delicate flavours of Norman *fromage*, they can watch the huge ships passing out to the estuary.

The town is a weekend retreat for the Rouennais, but its heyday was toward the end of the nineteenth century when it was immensely popular with the fashionable Paris set. The weekenders would come to La Bouille to enjoy the beautiful view and meander along the banks of the river Seine. During this period, the owner of a dairy at La Bouille, one Madame Dupuis, created an excellent cow's cheese that she named for the town. Madame famously sold her soft double-cream cheese on a bed of plane-tree leaves. The reputation of this cheese was so good that people came from miles around to buy enough to enjoy in their weekday houses until their next sojourn in the country.

Normandy's rich soil and fertile pastures make it prime dairy country. The fat, happy Norman cows, coupled with a cheese-making tradition that dates back to the dark ages, makes Normandy's status as France's leading cheese-producing region unsurprising.

The Normans have been making Camembert for centuries, at least as early as 1680. Camembert is made from raw cow's milk, which after it has been curdled and hand-ladled into moulds, is ripened by covering the curds with a layer of penicillin. The ripening process must last at least three weeks; the cheese is said to be à *point* when it is between thirty and thirty-five days old. When Camembert is young it is quite firm and crumbly, but as the cheese ages inside its supple crust it becomes viscous and velvety. There are strict regulations to protect the quality of Norman Camembert: it must be made of raw, unfiltered milk from cows that have been fed under strict conditions, and the overall fat content of the cheese must be 38 per cent. The cheese *gendarmes* insist that if pasteurised milk is used in the production, the result may be cheese, but it certainly isn't Camembert.

Locally it is said that one can tell that Camembert is ripe when it 'squeezes like a woman's breast'. One of my kids cheekily commented that it was likely that lots of men would say that they were experts in this area. There is a slightly more reliable test for the ideal Camembert, but this can only be done once the cheese has been purchased – cut into the cheese and look at the width of the layer between the crusts. If the layer is as thick as a knife blade,

the Camembert is said to be in perfect condition. If the layer is thicker than a knife blade, the cheese is too young and will be brittle and tasteless. If there is hardly any layer at all, the Camembert is over-ripe and may be runny and smell of ammonia – it certainly won't be at its best. It is said that the melting clocks in Dali's 'The Persistence of Memory' were inspired by a too-mature Camembert's dribbly insides.

I rely heavily on my favourite *fromagerie* in Rouen to instruct me in the matters of cheese, such as which cheese to buy in which season, and they have yet to steer me wrong. In terms of trust they are up there with the local priest. I have been told by Monsieur always to store my Camembert upside-down to preserve its beautiful shape. I am also told that the very best Camembert is produced in late spring and early summer when you get a lush, grassy flavour. Monsieur is also adamant that fridges are the enemy of cheese. He's got a point: refrigeration stifles the flavour. I tend to buy cheese for eating that day – only enough for a particular meal – so as to avoid having to refrigerate it.

Discovering nuances of flavour or cooking technique in Norman cuisine often came as the result of a happy accident. One hot Sunday our family visited Fécamp, a Norman seaside village, for a morning of picnicking and swimming. After lunch, we took a stroll through the narrow cobblestone streets and found ourselves standing outside a magnificent building, the Palais de Bénédictine. As luck would have it, we had stumbled upon one of the region's most visited attractions. That afternoon we got a fascinating insight into the history of distillation and we left Fécamp with a better appreciation of a peculiarly Norman flavour – Bénédictine.

Fécamp Abbey - home of Bénédictine.

Dom Bernado Vincelli, a monk of the Fécamp Abbey, used a complex and lengthy distillation process to transform a bitter medicinal liquid made of twenty-seven exotic herbs and roots into a delicious 'elixir of health'. This elixir was said to have healing properties and was most useful for sparking up listless monks. The liqueur was also highly regarded by the court of King François I: 'On my word, gentlemen. I have never tasted better,' His Majesty was heard to pronounce after taking a swig. Dom Vincelli's brothers continued making the drink right up until the end of the eighteenth century when, in the tumult of the French Revolution, the monks were dispersed and the formula disappeared.

A wine merchant by the name of Alexandre Le Grand unearthed the recipe in 1863. He modified the original recipe slightly using herbs and spices such as coriander, thyme, juniper berries, fruit peel and saffron. The present-day Bénédictine liqueur, sweet and aromatic in taste, is often taken after dinner. The recipe for it is, of course, top secret, and indeed is kept hidden in three different locations across the world to avoid it going the same way as the original recipe. It's comforting to know that even in the case of global catastrophe we will still be able to drown our sorrows in a glass of Bénédictine.

Savoir-faire

One morning I entered the *boulangerie* on the main street of Bourg-Achard to buy a loaf of bread, as I did every day. I only narrowly avoided colliding with a diminutive, well-dressed *dame d'un certain âge*. Madame came to a sudden halt, peered over her spectacles and austerely looked me up and down, before murmuring a salutation with patrician disdain. This woman had the demeanour of one who knows her own opinions, and what's more knows that *they are always right*. As I timidly returned her greeting, she continued her inspection of me, scrutinising me with the critical eye of a gallery owner overseeing the installation of a new artwork. Her eyes narrowed.

'You are the Australian from Château de Bosgouet.' It was a statement rather than an enquiry. The artwork was obviously hanging lopsidedly.

A half whispered '*Oui, Madame*' was about all I could manage. Had I unwittingly offended her? Was I about to get a dressing down from this curiously stern woman?

'You have children,' she informed me in such a way that I probably would not have disputed it even if she'd been wrong.

I nodded fervently. She had obviously done a bit of scouting; she knew that I had four children and indeed their approximate ages.

'I really must apologise,' she continued with sudden warmth. 'I have driven past Bosgouet so many times and keep meaning to drop in to welcome you, and yet . . .' Madame trailed off with that ambiguous shrug that finishes so many French sentences.

I was taken aback at this change in tone. Madame Chantal went on to introduce herself formally and invite me and *mes enfants* to her nearby château the following afternoon for *le goûter* (afternoon tea). She explained that three of her grandchildren were staying with her; she thought it would be nice for the children to meet, and for us to take tea.

'We can sit and talk. We might enjoy one another's company, or we might not. We shall see.'

With that, she nodded firmly, indicating the end of the conversation and went on her way up the road.

Sometimes I profess myself baffled by the behaviour of the French. Often what can be misconstrued as rudeness or arrogance is in fact simply candour – and it's quite refreshing once you become accustomed to it. On reflection the frankness of Madame's assessment of the possibility – or not – of friendship between us was actually endearing. Why waste time sweet talking? That said, the French are absolute sticklers for formal social conventions – *politesse* (courtesy) – and I was forever in fear of breaking some unknown code that would see me kicked out of the club. In France *savoir-faire* (tact; literally, to know how to act) is the best trait you could possibly display.

There are myriad complex rules that govern all social interactions in France. The most important ones seem to orbit around greeting people and, unsurprisingly, dining habits. The use of polite language is sacrosanct. Always greet people using both a salutation (*bonjour*, *bonsoir*) and a title (*Madame*, *Monsieur*). Don't start a conversation in English no matter how desperately poor your French is. Watch your use of the informal pronoun *tu*; over-familiarity is seldom tolerated. As for dining, always keep your hands above the table. Wait for the host's toast before quaffing your aperitif. If you're invited to dinner, bring a gift – a *good* bottle of wine, absolutely no cheap plonk – or arrange for flowers to be sent earlier in the day. These are only a few basic rules. Have no illusions about it, French etiquette is a minefield and not following these codes can lead you down a frosty path indeed.

The children and I did visit Château de Hautonne, where Madame Chantal was waiting for us with her three immaculately dressed grandsons. *Le goûter* was laid out in the garden next to cushions and chairs that were arranged just so. The children played and swam in the pool as Madame and I talked politely. My conversation was a little stilted as I mentally edited out any comments that I thought might cause offence. I was very keen to make a good impression. I cannot say that we two became the best of friends, but we stopped to have a chat whenever we bumped into one another. I felt more assured with each meeting. I'd enquire about her grandchildren and she in turn would enquire about my kids. Who knows? With time this reserved exchange may develop into a true friendship, and I may master French *politesse* yet.

Cheese

Though it's the best-known of Normandy's cheese family, Camembert has a few competitors when it comes to my affections. Livarot, a washed-rind cow's-milk cheese, has a full-bodied flavour and a not-unpleasant pungent smell. It is known by the moniker 'the little colonel' because the cheese is dressed in bands of raffia that resemble the stripes on a French colonel's sleeve. Livarot is aged in cool, damp cellars and this gives its rind a lovely burnt-orange colour.

Pont-l'Évêque is square-shaped with golden-yellow insides encased in a cross-hatched tan-coloured rind. Its taste is rich and tangy, but is milder than that of Livarot.

And then there is the Neufchâtel, a soft, unripened cheese with a flowered, bloomy rind. It is spreadable like cream cheese but has a curiously grainy texture. When young it has a salty but delicate flavour that becomes more indelicate with age; leave it for too long and Neufchâtel will taste quite sour. Even though Neufchâtel can be a bit temperamental, I forgive it because of its pretty heart shape — it looks irresistible on a cheese platter.

Learning to cook at Bosgouet

I knew from the start that it would have been too ambitious to try to run The French Table in the first year we were in Normandy. We had only really just settled in to the château and the village. It would have been madness to try to pass myself off as an expert on the region when I was so new to the neighbourhood. More to the point, I wanted to make sure I was doing everything properly, not hastily cobbling together something that would be second rate. So, in our first summer at Bosgouet I spent time refining my plan for The French Table.

My role would be as impresario. I would play host to the groups of guests who had come to Bosgouet to get a taste of the château life and learn to cook. The groups would stay for a week at a time, and I'd put together an itinerary that would take in the sights of Normandy as well as the region's best markets and restaurants. I wanted a well-reputed chef to run daily hands-on cooking classes, using ingredients that would either come from our potager or from the local markets we visited.

Many of the talented chefs I'd had the pleasure to work with had become great friends and I was impatient to be back in the kitchen with them again. However, the choice of which chef to bring on board was critical. I needed someone who had a passion for their craft and was able to impart that passion to the eager students. This is not as straightforward as it sounds; great culinary skill does not always equate with being a good teacher. I started to draw up a shortlist of chefs who I knew would be both patient and interesting teachers.

Sorting out the nuts and bolts of the business – budgets, models, marketing strategies, and setting up our website – was demanding work. I also had

Making gnocchi.

to figure out exactly how many guests I could cater for at one time. I would be cooking all their meals, keeping up with their laundry and housekeeping needs, as well as escorting them as a guide around the region. It was clear that either I could only take on one or two small, uncomplaining and exceptionally clean guests or else employ some people to give me a hand. Many young people from across the Channel flock to Normandy during the summer, hoping to refine their French. I asked a few locals about the summer workforce. It was clear that it would be relatively easy to find a few Brits who'd be keen for some part-time work making beds and laundering sheets.

I grappled with my sums for insurance, supplies and wages. Much more pleasurable than staring at the figures that made up my budgets was my 'gruelling' research – talking with local cooks about traditional French fare. I was graciously invited into many kitchens. There, I was impressed by people's generosity with their time and knowledge. There was no jealous guarding of recipes or techniques. One of my first Norman cooking research missions was in the rural kitchen of L'Amandier in Bourg-Achard. Chef Frederik had invited me to learn how to make his dreamy version of sabayon, a decadent emulsion of eggs, sugar, cream and vanilla served simply with the strawberries picked fresh from Frederik's potager.

Frederik also introduced me to the French cook's rite of passage: cooking foie gras. The French are extremely protective of what they consider to be the bastion of their culinary culture and have famously resisted pressure from other European countries to halt the force-feeding of ducks and geese to increase the size of the animals' livers.

In typical Gallic fashion Frederik was completely unfazed by handling duck's innards. I was initially a bit squeamish, but I reasoned that if I was willing to eat it, I should be willing to get my hands dirty. Frederik showed me the whole duck liver, pointing out the filaments, nerves and sinew. These are bitter tasting and will ruin the smooth taste and silky texture of the foie gras if not expertly removed.

Frederik plonked the pale-coloured liver on a board, carefully prised apart the two lobes and with a filleting knife removed the sinew. He then placed the liver in a long rectangular cast-iron terrine mould, seasoned it with salt and pepper, and flavoured it with an unmeasured splash of Madeira. Frederik covered the terrine mould with a layer of foil, placed it in a water bath and cooked it in the oven for an hour and a half.

After he had unveiled the cooked foie gras with a flourish, Frederik left me with stern instructions to serve it with fresh fig confiture and a glass of Sauterne; the foie gras is a natural partner to this famous wine. I loved Frederik's manner; he was so sure-footed in the kitchen and had a great sense of traditionally Norman taste pairings. I hoped to use him as a consultant throughout the course of my preparations.

Everything was slowly coming together. I had a firm plan for how The French Table would run, and my research into cuisine was going along well. Now all I had to do was find the guests.

Summer recipes

Mussels with Chilli, Ginger and Garlic

Mussels are terrifically easy to cook – perfect for a no-fuss summer dinner. These beauties make a great alternative to fish and chips Serves 4.

INGREDIENTS

olive oil, for cooking
3 cloves garlic, finely chopped
2 cm piece ginger, finely chopped
1 fresh small red chilli, chopped
1 cup dry white wine
1 kg black mussels, scrubbed
    and cleaned
2 spring onions, thinly sliced
2 tablespoons finely chopped
    flat-leaf parsley
French fries and baguettes,
    to serve

METHOD

Heat a heavy-based saucepan over low heat for 1–2 minutes. Brush base lightly with olive oil. Gently cook garlic, ginger and chilli for 1 minute. Add wine and 1 cup water, then increase heat to medium and bring to the boil. Add mussels and spring onions. Cook covered for 3–5 minutes or until mussels open. Discard any unopened mussels.

Sprinkle mussels with parsley. Serve with French fries and baguettes to mop up the lovely sauce.

Stuffed Tomatoes

The breadcrumbs give these little 'bombs', as Alex likes to call them, a contrasting crunch. Serve with a green salad or as an accompaniment to a chicken dish. Serves 6–8.

INGREDIENTS

6 ripe tomatoes
1 onion, finely chopped
6 rashers (slices) bacon, chopped
1 clove garlic, finely chopped
½ cup olive oil
⅓ cup chopped basil
½ cup freshly grated Parmesan
1 cup fresh breadcrumbs
sea salt and freshly ground
   black pepper

METHOD

Preheat oven to 180° (350°F).

Wash and dry tomatoes, then cut in half widthwise and spoon out the seeds. Blot the tomatoes dry using kitchen paper, and then place tomato halves cut-side up in an 18 x 26 cm baking dish.

Sauté onion, bacon and garlic in ¼ cup of the olive oil in a frying pan over low heat for 6–8 minutes. Combine 2 tablespoons of the olive oil, basil, Parmesan and breadcrumbs with onion, bacon and garlic mixture, then season to taste. Divide stuffing between the tomato halves, and then drizzle remaining olive oil over the tops of the tomatoes.

Bake tomatoes for 25–30 minutes or until filling is crisp and golden. Serve hot.

Eye Fillets with Béarnaise Sauce

This classic French sauce, an emulsion of egg yolks into butter, is characterised by its vinegar and tarragon flavours. It is a natural partner to steak but goes well with any grilled meat. Serves 6.

INGREDIENTS

1 tablespoon butter
6 x 2 cm-thick beef eye fillets
30 ml dry sherry

Béarnaise Sauce
¼ cup tarragon vinegar
¼ cup apple cider
2 golden shallots, finely chopped
¼ cup French tarragon,
   finely chopped
sea salt and freshly ground
   black pepper
3 egg yolks
180 g butter, chopped into cubes

METHOD

For the Béarnaise sauce, boil vinegar, cider, shallots and 1 tablespoon of the chopped tarragon in a small saucepan over medium heat for about 5–10 minutes or until there is ¼ cup remaining. Season to taste.

In a bowl over boiling water, beat egg yolks, then beat into the cider and vinegar mixture. Add 1 tablespoon of the butter. Cook over very low heat for 1–2 minutes; do not let the sauce boil or the egg yolks will curdle.

Add the remaining butter to the mixture a cube at a time and continue to beat with a whisk until butter melts and is incorporated. Whisk in remaining tarragon. Keep warm.

Melt butter in a cast-iron frying pan over high heat. Sear steaks on both sides until brown. Pour in sherry, then cook for another 5 minutes for rare or until cooked to your liking. Transfer to a warm platter.

Serve at once with Béarnaise sauce passed separately. *Bon appetit!*

Snapper Fillets with Almonds

The succulent flesh of the red snapper soaks up the lemon juice, giving it a fresh, clean taste. An easy recipe for lazy summer evenings. Serves 4.

INGREDIENTS

4 x 200 g snapper fillets, skin
  removed and pin-boned
rice flour, for dusting
sea salt and freshly ground
  black pepper
¼ cup olive oil
½ cup slivered almonds
120 g butter, melted
juice of 1 lemon
2 tablespoons chopped
  flat-leaf parsley
green salad, to serve

METHOD

Preheat oven to 190°C (375°F).

Lightly coat snapper fillets with flour and season to taste.

Heat olive oil in a frying pan over high heat, add snapper and cook for 2–3 minutes or until they are browned on both sides.

Lay the fillets in a large baking dish and pour over a mixture of slivered almonds, melted butter, lemon juice, parsley and a little black pepper. Bake for 10 minutes or until almonds are golden and toasted.

Serve snapper fillets and almonds immediately with a fresh green salad.

Pommes Charlotte Salad

This is inspired by Martha Stewart's well-known recipe for potato salad, although I have used raspberry vinegar in place of wine vinegar, omitted the cornichons and added bacon and a little mustard. Serves 4–6.

INGREDIENTS

15–20 potatoes (in France I like to use tiny charlotte potatoes, but you could use chat potatoes or other small new potatoes)
sea salt
¼ cup Vermouth
4 rashers bacon, fat and rind trimmed
1 tablespoon raspberry vinegar
1 teaspoon caster (superfine) sugar
¾ cup crème fraîche
1 tablespoon whole-egg mayonnaise
1 teaspoon wholegrain mustard
freshly ground black pepper
1 bunch spring onions, thinly sliced on the diagonal
½ cup chopped flat-leaf parsley

METHOD

Place potatoes in a large saucepan, then add salt and bring to the boil over high heat. Reduce heat to low and simmer for 2 minutes or until potatoes are just tender when tested with a fork. Remove from heat, drain, and sprinkle with Vermouth. Leave to stand until cool.

Pan-fry bacon rashers on medium heat for a few minutes each side. Remove from heat, leave to cool, then cut into small pieces.

Whisk together the vinegar, sugar, crème fraîche, mayonnaise and mustard. Season to taste. Add bacon pieces to the dressing.

Cut potatoes into bite-sized pieces and transfer to a serving bowl. Pour dressing over the potatoes. Sprinkle with spring onions and parsley, then toss to combine. Adjust seasoning.

Serve at room temperature.

Raspberry Tart

This gorgeous lattice tart, based on a recipe from the July 2005 issue of American magazine *Gourmet*, will impress any guest. Serves 10–12.

INGREDIENTS

egg yolk, lightly beaten
crème fraîche, to serve

Pastry
1½ cups plain (all-purpose) flour
80 g caster (superfine) sugar
¼ teaspoon salt
125 g butter, diced, plus extra,
  for greasing
2 egg yolks
2–3 tablespoons iced water

Raspberry Filling
500 g raspberries
½ cup white sugar
2 tablespoons plain
  (all-purpose) flour

METHOD

For pastry, using a food processor, combine dry ingredients with the butter by pulsing mixture until it's crumbly. Pour in whisked egg yolks and water and pulse until all ingredients come together. Roll the dough into a ball, wrap in plastic film and refrigerate for at least half an hour.

Preheat oven to 180°C (350°F). Brush a 22 cm tart tin with a removable base with melted butter.

Roll out three-quarters of the pastry in a 3 mm-thick round. Press dough gently into the tart tin, trim edges and prick all over base of shell lightly with a fork.

Blind bake for 20–25 minutes or until pastry is golden. Leave in tin to cool.

Meanwhile, for the raspberry filling, place raspberries, sugar and flour in a heavy-based saucepan, and stir to combine. Simmer over medium heat, stirring, for about 5 minutes or until raspberries collapse and liquid from berries is thickened. Remove from heat and cool completely. $\longrightarrow$

Berry-hunting is a favourite summer pastime in Normandy.

Spread raspberry filling evenly over the pastry.

Roll out remaining pastry ball and cut into 1.5 cm-thick strips. Lay pastry strips 1 cm apart across raspberry filling, pressing ends onto edge of crust. Arrange more strips across to form a lattice pattern. Trim edges of all strips to edge of the tin. Brush pastry lattice with beaten egg yolk.

Bake tart for 25–30 minutes or until pastry lattice is golden. Cool in tin on a wire rack for 10 minutes, then remove side of pan and leave to cool.

Serve slices of warm or room temperature tart topped with dollops of crème fraîche.

Tarte au Citron

This dessert is another staple of French cuisine. The perfect *tarte au citron* will have a crisp, biscuity and not-too-heavy base, and a full-tasting, tangy filling. Serves 12.

INGREDIENTS

icing sugar, for dusting

Almond Pastry
185 g plain (all-purpose) flour
⅓ cup ground almonds
1 tablespoon caster
    (superfine) sugar
1 teaspoon finely grated
    lemon zest
160 g butter, chopped
1–2 tablespoons iced water

Lemon Filling
3 eggs
150 g caster (superfine) sugar
finely grated zest and juice of
    2 large lemons
150 g unsalted butter, melted
50 g ground almonds

METHOD

For almond pastry, pulse together flour, ground almonds, sugar and lemon zest in a food processor until combined. Add chopped butter and pulse until most of mixture resembles coarse breadcrumbs with some small lumps of butter. Drizzle 1–2 tablespoons iced water into flour mixture and pulse until dough just forms a ball. Wrap in plastic film, then chill in the refrigerator for 1 hour or until firm.

Roll pastry out on a lightly floured bench, then use to line a greased 24 cm tart tin with a removable base. Chill in the refrigerator for at least 1 hour.

Preheat oven to 190°C (375°F). Line tart shell with baking paper, then add pastry weights and bake for 15 minutes. Remove baking paper and pastry weights and cook for another 10 minutes or until golden and dry. Leave to cool on a wire rack. Reduce oven temperature to 170°C (340°F).

Meanwhile, for the filling, whisk eggs with sugar, lemon zest and half of the juice. Add butter, remaining lemon juice and ground almonds and stir to combine.

Pour lemon filling into pastry shell, then bake for 40 minutes or until lemon filling sets. Leave to cool on a wire rack. Dust with icing sugar and serve.

Blackberry Butter Cake

In the summertime plump blackberries grow in abundance all over the
Norman countryside. The kids loved to go blackberry picking, and this cake
was one of my favourite ways of using the spoils of their hunts.
Serves 8–10.

INGREDIENTS

250 g unsalted butter, at room
    temperature, chopped
½ cup caster (superfine) sugar
2 large eggs
2 cups plain (all-purpose) flour
½ teaspoon baking powder
¼ teaspoon bicarbonate of soda
⅓ cup milk
200 g blackberries
icing sugar, for dusting

METHOD

Preheat oven to 180°C (350°F). Butter and flour an
18 cm springform cake pan and set aside.

In a mixing bowl, beat butter, sugar and eggs until
thick and creamy. Add sifted flour, baking powder,
bicarbonate of soda and milk. Beat until smooth.
Fold the blackberries through.

Spread mixture in the pan. Bake for 35 minutes or
until cake is pale golden and springs back when
pressed in the centre.

Cool on a wire rack. Loosen edges with a knife and
push out of pan.

Dust cake generously with icing sugar and serve.

Lemon Curd

Makes about 2 cups.

INGREDIENTS

finely grated zest and strained
  juice of 4 lemons
450 g granulated white sugar
110 g unsalted butter, chopped
4 eggs, lightly beaten

METHOD

Put lemon zest and juice, sugar,
butter and beaten eggs into a
large heatproof bowl over a pan
of simmering water; make sure
that bowl does not touch water.
Stir with a wooden spoon until
mixture is thick and coats the back
of the spoon. Pour into 2 x 250 ml
warm sterilised jars, then cover
and seal.

Lemon curd will keep in
the refrigerator for 1 week
after opening and up to
1 month unopened.

Jonquay Cocktail

Mix 2 parts Calvados, 2 parts lemon juice and 1 part Cointreau and shake vigorously in a cocktail shaker with loads of ice. Pour mixture into sugar-rimmed champagne flutes and serve.

La vie française
(french life)

We would always call on the children to help out with jobs on the château's grounds, and these tasks changed with the seasons. In autumn we cleared fallen wood from the forests and stacked it up for our fires. If we had had a night's worth of good rain, the next day there were mushrooms to dig out from the rich soil.

Mushroom hunting is a favourite pastime of the French. Go outside early any October morning and you'll see many families, baskets in hand, looking for *girolles*, *cèpes* and other wild species. Unlike these families, we were not *au fait* with the local varieties of fungi, edible or otherwise. One of the locals, Monsieur Antoine, a gruff but kind elderly fellow, the village's resident mycologist, generously offered to give us some tips. Monsieur joined us on an expedition. He broke a long branch off a tree and handed it to Alex, showing her how she could use the stick to unearth mushrooms. He examined each example we uncovered to confirm that it was *comestible* (edible) before putting it in our basket. We had a back-up for times when Monsieur Antoine could not join us on our hunt: the pharmacy in the next village. In France every pharmacist must pass a fungi identification exam. It is common to see people bringing their finds into the local chemist to check whether they are good to eat.

The kids loved gathering chestnuts and piling them in the cool, dark larder, ready to be transformed into a warming, creamy chestnut soup. Autumn also gave us crunchy pears and apples, and these were carefully transported back to the house in baskets by all four Webster children. From the orchard to the kitchen bench, the last of the peaches and plums were stewed and stored in readiness for the winter ahead.

On autumn afternoons – once the chores had been done – the kids would take walks, go on bike rides, play card-games in front of a roaring fire, or read while lying under a blanket on a sofa. Meanwhile I would tap away at my laptop, finessing The French Table's website and answering the enquiries that were trickling in. I had finally settled on a chef for the inaugural session: Marieke Brugman of Howqua Dale Gourmet Retreat in Victoria. Marieke is a superb chef with a great feeling for French cuisine. Having studied under her myself, I knew Marieke to be a patient and kind teacher. I also considered how nice it would be to have a friendly face around during what I was predicting to be an anxious time. It felt satisfying to be bedding down all these details.

Mushroom hunting.

One gorgeous autumn afternoon I was sitting in the sitting room drafting an email to Marieke about possible menus for the cooking classes. Outside the neighbourhood farmers were tending their fields, tilling them to prepare them for winter. I knew that in nearby orchards apples would be ready and waiting to be picked; the trees bowed with the weight of the fruit. I looked up from the laptop to see two unexpected visitors strolling down the château's long driveway. It was in this fashion that John and Libby Wolfe walked into our lives. John rang the bell and when I answered it he greeted me in a broad St Louis accent. 'Well, I heard that Australians had bought Château de Bosgouet, and I just had to come to see for myself.'

I never knew that we Australians were such fascinating creatures!

There were handshakes all round and I invited John and his wife, Libby, to join us for tea that very afternoon. So began our friendship. John and Libby, who are now in their eighties, had moved to Normandy with their three children some forty years before when John was seconded by his firm to head up a French branch of the business. They are an outgoing couple who are generous with their time. Actually this is understating it – they are social dynamos and they have seemingly boundless energy to devote to both old and new friendships. John always has a wonderfully wry anecdote or two at the ready, and Libby has the warmest-sounding laugh you could imagine. This makes them much sought-after dinner companions, and they are fixtures on invitation lists for almost every event in the region. John and Libby have a genuine love for the area and know it back to front – from the finest restaurants to the best person from whom to buy a tractor, even the surest method of eradicating moles.

Through John we not only got to know many locals much better, but we were also introduced to other *étrangers* – those who, like us, had been captivated by the French countryside and had bought properties in the region.

It was evident that we were gradually moving from the status of newcomers to something else. We would never be graced with the title of 'locals' – this coveted label eluded those who had moved to the village over forty years before us. Some of the people of Bosgouet were still perplexed that these Australian interlopers had moved next door, but they were kind and welcoming, often inviting us into their homes for an aperitif or a cup of tea. Our children were invited to all the village birthday parties, and we in turn invited the local kids over for play dates, movie nights and bonfires. While customs differ, children are children and some behaviours transcend cultural barriers. This means that parents the world over will always be kept awake by giggles and squeals during sleepovers.

The friendships that we developed at Bosgouet were quite unexpected. We really did not know if we would make any friends during our stay in France. I spent a lot of time considering how the fruit and vegetables of the region flourish, but how friendships grow is altogether a harder thing to fathom.

Libby and John, our fellow interlopers, join us for tea and a slice of apple cake.

Fleur de sel

I am seldom taken in by food fashions, but I admit to being a touch smitten with the current trend for specialty salts. It's not that I'm swayed by the exotic origins of these products or by claims that the salt flakes were painstakingly raked by lithe, shirtless men; it's simply a matter of superiority of flavour. A quick dip into the vast array of 'new' seasonings — black salt from India, Halen Mon from north Wales, Maldon from England — and you'll never go back to astringent, chemical-laden table salt.

Normandy is home to the top-of-the-line boutique salt — fleur de sel *(flower of salt). The mere mention of its name will make a gourmet's heart beat a little faster. The moist grey crystals of* fleur de sel *have a delicate, sweet but identifiably oceanic taste. Its crystalline form means that it does not dissolve as quickly as other types of salt; instead* fleur de sel *crunches satisfyingly between your teeth.*

The fleur de sel *crystals 'bloom' on the surface of shallow saltwater marshes in Guerande, Normandy. These crystals are then skimmed off the top of the pools by hand, leaving below the less pure, but more affordable,* sel gris *(grey salt, so named because of the clay particles that give it its colour). For every 35 kilos of* sel gris *harvested, there will be only half a kilo of* fleur de sel *produced. Its rarity affects the price —* fleur de sel *is expensive, but you only need a few of the pretty, lacy crystals to transform the blandest of dishes into something spectacular.*

The French style is to add fleur de sel *to sweet things to balance the flavours. Try it on a slice of melon!*

La foire à tout in La Bouille.

An auction house in Elbeuf

I have vivid childhood memories of my parents intently scouring the Melbourne papers for local and rural auctions and estate sales. They were dedicated antique hunters. Each Saturday morning I'd stumble out of bed to see them sitting at a kitchen table covered by the weekend classifieds. Their red pens would be poised, ready to circle any exciting prospect. We would often spend the whole weekend trawling antique shops across Victoria, looking in dusty backrooms for that next elusive piece.

Pete and I caught the same bug early on in our marriage. We were both keen to decorate Château de Bosgouet with locally found treasures. With the same fanaticism as my parents had shown all those years ago, we screeched to a stop whenever we passed an advertisement for a local auction. We jumped out of the car to eagerly scrawl down the date and location.

One Sunday morning in early autumn Pete and I had gone for a drive to the nearby village of Elbeuf. As we were wandering the streets in search of strong coffee, we came upon a poster advertising a newly opened antique auction house. We followed the arrows on the poster and ventured down a medieval cobblestone laneway into a tiny but beautifully manicured courtyard. We knocked on an old oak door at the back of the courtyard. The door creaked open and we were politely greeted by the proprietor of the auction house. Monsieur, a smooth-looking, impeccably dressed young man, ushered us inside. He introduced himself as a Parisian who had left the capital in search of *objets d'art*. He said that Normandy was a rich source. He led us through a small office, which was a shambles of papers and files, into his showroom, a dilapidated old warehouse space full of Louis XIV-period furniture – items of such beauty that I could only clutch dumbly at Pete's hand.

Happening upon that poster proved providential. We spent many an auction day (always a Sunday) in Monsieur's cobblestone courtyard, bidding as if our lives depended on it. The competition was always fierce because Monsieur is a young man of exceptional taste who only auctions pieces of quality. We vied for these pieces against the packs of smartly dressed Parisians who travel to their Normandy *maisons secondaires* on the weekends. This weekender crowd is made up of particularly intractable bidders who will not give in without a fight. We have been lucky enough to pick up a number of choice pieces from this auction house, including two French bronze mantelclocks and a huge, brightly coloured *tapis* (rug), but we've had some real disappointments, too. We missed out on a stunning pair of occasional chairs to a middle-aged woman who would just not be outbid, even though the prices soared high above the reserve.

The French auction system works exactly as it does in Australia. The pieces that are to be sold are displayed for a period of time before auction day, giving the potential buyer enough time to examine any objects before they go under the hammer. One Saturday I was looking over the contents of Monsieur's showroom before the next day's auction. I caught sight of an elegant *chaise* (chair) sitting slightly askew in front of a large glass display cabinet. I liked the look of the *chaise*, but I gave a little gasp when I saw the contents of the cabinet behind it. On the centre shelf sat two black Hermès Kelly bags: one vintage, the other looking almost new.

The Kelly bag had its debut in 1956 when Grace Kelly used an oversized crocodile-hide handbag, made by the legendary French luxury goods house Hermès, to hide her pregnancy. There is something about the Kelly bag that makes it ineffably French; it is stylish, discreet, outlandishly expensive and famously unavailable. After spying these two confections, I was unable to

ACHAT DE TOUTES
ANTIQUITES

MEUBLES - BIBELOTS
OBJETS ANCIENS
MIROIRS - PENDULES

SUCCESSION
DEBARRAS

concentrate on the *chaise* or indeed anything else. I was preoccupied with inspecting the *sacs* (bags) – examining the hides, the gleaming hardware, the tiny padlocks – while Peter concerned himself with the far more practical job of assessing the *chaise* for flaws in its upholstery.

Pete asked me what I thought of the *chaise*, whether I thought the tapestry was a little too worn, but it was no good; I was transfixed by the bags and could not get my mouth to shape any words other than 'Kelly' and 'handbag'. After upbraiding me for not paying attention to the task at hand, Pete rolled his eyes and suggested I find out the reserve prices on the *chaise* and the bags. He could tell I was a lost cause. I raced over to Monsieur. I was more interested in the new Hermès bag than the vintage one. I was imagining what good company the black beauty would be as we both aged when Monsieur came back with the reserve: a quarter of the retail price!

'Oh, and the reserve on that chair, too,' I said, pointing vaguely in the direction of Pete. Monsieur looked through his list and gave me the reserve on the *chaise*.

'I 'ope you 'ave more luck than you did at the last auction on that pair of chairs,' Monsieur offered kindly. 'Madame who bid against you wanted the chairs very much. They were part of her uncle's estate, and she was not going to stop until she bought them . . . Your 'usband made her pay for them, though.'

I nodded as I remembered the scene, then raised both hands, palms up and shrugged in that oh-so-French gesture that suggests a cool aloofness — an essential play in the game of the auction. I said *à bientôt* to Monsieur and returned to Peter to relay all the information, before reluctantly leaving the auction house.

The next day dawned. I remembered that we had promised the children a Sunday lunch in a restaurant in Rouen, so we rang up the auction house and left absentee bids on the items. Our experience over the years has shown this to be an excellent way to buy at auction, helping us to avoid the temptation of going over the agreed price and emptying our pockets. Bids sorted, we headed off for lunch at Rouen's famous La Couronne restaurant, located in the Vieux-Marché. This Rouennaise institution is France's oldest *auberge*, and has been serving food since 1345. Over a classic rural lunch of French onion soup, steak and *frites*, a plate of cheese and large, flat ceramic dishes filled with that creamy toffee concoction crème brûlée, we wondered if our bids had been successful. A few sips of Château Roquegrave, a fine Bordeaux, helped to quieten the anxiety I felt.

On our way home that afternoon we saw roadside signs advertising a *foire à tout* at La Bouille.

My new friend, a Hermès Kelly bag found at an auction house.

'What is a *foire à tout*?' I wondered out loud.

'A fair of all,' replied Millie from the back seat of the car — it never ceased to amaze me how fluent the children were becoming. They were fast outpacing their parents. We decided to take a detour to see for ourselves.

Winding our way down from the *route nationale*, along a picturesque forest road to the banks of the Seine, we were all excited to see what this 'fair of all' entailed. We made our final descent and turned left into the little village that we had grown to love for its magnificent restaurants, art galleries and artisans' studios.

The *foire à tout* was a huge trash and treasure market with dozens of stalls selling everything from books to pieces of furniture.

Our coterie began to scour the stalls. The vendors expect their customers to haggle over the pieces even though they are already very low in price. That day at La Bouille I bought a turn-of-the-century copper fire-jug with a blue-and-white china handle for the bargain price of 2 euros. I also picked up a couple of stamped Quimperware bowls in perfect condition for only 50 centimes each. Quimperware is hand-painted French pottery, named for the town of Quimper in Brittany. A few days later I entered a very smart antiquarian store in Rouen to find an almost identical Quimperware bowl selling for 125 euros; the only difference was that the latter came with a chip! We went home, new finds under our arms, feeling quite pleased with ourselves for having stopped off to visit the *foire à tout*. In the months that followed we attended many of these village fairs and became the new owners of many treasures: copper pots, china kitchenware, leatherbound books and wicker baskets.

As for our absentee bids, we received a phone call the next morning to say we had been successful with the *chaise*, a solid-pine kitchen *armoire* and, yes, I would have a new friend with which I could grow old gracefully!

Calvados

Distilled cider has a long tradition in Normandy. The first written references date from the sixteenth century, long before the cider took the name of Calvados. The first distillation of cider yields an intermediate product, the petites eaux, *which has an alcoholic content of about 30 per cent proof. The heads and tails, which contain undesirable compounds, are carefully eliminated.*

These petites eaux *are then heated for the second distillation, the* bonne chauffe. *The heads and tails are once again eliminated. At this stage the Calvados produced has a strength of 70 per cent proof.*

Calvados is colourless, produces a burning sensation on the palate, and gives off an aroma of fruit and alcohol. It is typically served over an apple sorbet between courses to clear the palate and aid digestion before the next course. This tradition is called le trou Normand, *or 'the Norman hole'.*

The markets of Normandy

When we were in Normandy a significant portion of our lives was ruled by our visits to local farmers markets – I could always tell what day of the week it was by which market I was at. Almost every village in France has a weekly market and each village market will have a few specialities; it is worth spending the time to explore which areas excel with which type of produce. You'll be in good company; going from market to market to try to track down the very best seasonal produce is practically a national sport.

MONDAY   After the weekend, the pantry at Bosgouet was usually looking pretty grim, so it was off to market in the next village, Bourg-Achard. Every Monday the farmers, butchers, flower sellers, upholsters, linen ladies and a horde of others gather in front of the picturesque *mairie*. I'd start the day with a *café crème* and a still-warm croissant in the JT Tabac. The Tabac is a hive of activity every day of the week, but even more so on bustling market Mondays. Elderly men gather at the bar to drink small glasses of Pernod Ricard – a favourite of the rural gentlemen – while ladies gather to chat over coffee, baskets brimming with market purchases at their feet. Even if I didn't need anything, I'd cycle the short distance to Bourg-Achard just to sit in the Tabac and soak up the atmosphere. That said, I hardly ever came home with an empty basket. My favourite things to buy were freshly roasted chickens and creamy ready-made potatoes dauphines.

TUESDAY   Of a Tuesday morning, it was only a short stroll to the end of the château's driveway to purchase all I needed for the day. Even tiny Bosgouet boasts its own *petit marché*, which consists of a single striped stand,

two jovial middle-aged farmers and produce that is second to none. These two fellows are always smiling and ready to impart some interesting tidbit about the produce that they're selling. These two farmers would simply bring to market whatever was ripe to pick from their own gardens. In autumn there were field mushrooms, which had a lovely nutty flavour, and boxes of apples – a different variety each week.

WEDNESDAY   Le Neubourg is a lively town that is host to a large live-stock market every Wednesday morning. This is one of the best and most authentic markets in Normandy and here you can buy anything from exotic Middle Eastern spices to quails. Hand-stuffed pork sausages are a speciality. It's quite a noisy market – full of the sounds of live animals and the chatter of bargain-hunters negotiating prices. At Le Neubourg there is little room for sentimentality: point out the squawking chicken you fancy taking home and the vendor will skilfully and quickly silence the bird on the spot. Not for the faint-hearted.

THURSDAY   Dieppe is said to have the finest food market in northern France. The quality of produce here is exceptional. Each Thursday at the place Church Saint-Jacques rubber-booted fishermen stand next to canopied stalls to sell that morning's catch. The Dieppe market has an endearingly chaotic feel to it: the salty smell of fresh fish mixes with the tangy scent of spices and that of steaming paella, which is cooked at stalls by the vat. The strains of the nearby merry-go-round compete with those of the buskers who line the foreshore, giving the place a slightly deranged-carnival feel. Smiling Arabic vendors sell spices that I cannot get at my usual shopping haunts – my absolute favourite is sumac. Also, look out for Monsieur Chevaucherie, a

Fresh seafood from the market in Dieppe.

coquilles
St Jacques
kg 4€60
4kg 18

Preparing le rosbif at Le Neubourg.

cuisinier traiteur who specialises in pastas. His special lasagne – filled with fresh snails and béchamel sauce – is out of this world.

FRIDAY   Nothing beats a leisurely Friday morning in Deauville before the Parisians arrive for the weekend. This village has a covered marketplace full of produce stalls with honey, jam and buttery foie gras – just for starters. Deauville is one of the best places to buy Calvados. There is also Madame Leufel with her exquisite quilts and Madame Vasse with soft cashmere jumpers, which she hand dyes.

SATURDAY   Honfleur is in the Norman department of Calvados, only a ten-minute drive from Bosgouet. Honfleur is located on the southern bank of the estuary of the river Seine, very close to the exit of the *Pont de Normandie* (Bridge of Normandy). The town is famous for its beautiful old port, and for its houses with their distinctive slate-covered frontages. These façades became synonymous with the *école de Honfleur*, the painting movement now considered a precursor to Impressionism. Artists in this school, in particular Gustave Courbet, Claude Monet and Johan Jongkind, painted these houses many times.

Every Saturday morning the entire town is preoccupied with the market. It is a hive of activity and the region's farmers use it as a chance to catch up on all the local gossip. It is primarily a food market, with eggs, cheese, butter, cream, chicken and seafood being of particularly good quality, but it also has artisans selling their wares, and there are even stalls selling designer footwear.

Down the road on the grounds of the Sainte-Catherine church – the largest wooden church in France – there is an organic fruit and vegetable market that would make any health-food guru salivate. On the other side of the Old Dock there is yet another market for fabrics, flower and various trades. We liked to arrive early and shop until lunch time, when we'd take a much-needed break to eat in one of the wonderful restaurants that sit beside the harbour.

SUNDAY   My favourite day of the week, and the day for the ultimate market experience: place Saint-Marc in Rouen. This bustling market includes *la brocante* (flea market) as well as fresh food stalls. We'd always start with coffee and a croque monsieur at one of the cafés near the market and then methodically work our way down every aisle. This market sells beautiful flowers and is home to many of the region's finest artisans. When I first arrived I did not know that our close neighbour Rouen was famous for the quality of its markets – it was a wonderful surprise!

A night in Paris

One morning the phone rang while I was preparing breakfast. I dusted off crumbs from the crusty baguette I'd been cutting and answered the phone.

'Jane!' an excitable voice called out. It was Jacquie, an old friend.

'Stop whatever it is you're doing. I'm in Paris and it's gorgeous . . . you have to join me in the city.'

At first I protested, envisaging the various disasters that could occur if I were to leave Pete and the kids to their own devices for twenty-four hours. But then I got over myself. Of course they'd be fine – and besides, who was I to say no to Paris?

A few hours later Pete waved me off at the train station. As the train pulled away and I settled in for the short 50-minute journey, I was suddenly energised by the idea of Jacquie and me having a Parisian sojourn. Our plans were to have dinner at the famous Café Marly, situated on a terrace overlooking the Louvre, and stay overnight in the nearby Hotel Bel Ami.

I alighted at Gare Saint-Lazare and winced at the idea of wrestling with my map. *No*, I thought. *I don't need the map; I'll smell my way to the left bank!* I took off on foot through the streets of Paris, my wheelie overnight bag gliding behind me and my nose leading the way. I felt as if my instincts had heightened significantly during my time in France. Because I wanted to take in every detail of these new sights, my wits became sharper, keener. I just didn't want any of it to pass me by.

Jacquie had suggested that we meet in the hotel lobby at 7 p.m., after she had wrapped up some business, so I found myself with a few precious hours to myself. I was proud that I was able to find the hotel without too much trouble. I checked in and stepped back out onto rue Saint-Benoît in the heart of Saint Germain. The Latin Quarter of Paris, my favourite quarter, is particularly lively. The air here is filled with the smells of espresso and baking bread. The nearby Sorbonne colours the atmosphere; students crowd the cafés, holding serious-looking discussions.

I brushed past a group of student-types who were gesticulating madly and made my way further down the boulevard to the church of Saint-Germain-des-Prés. Pete and I first visited this Benedictine abbey on our honeymoon. Every time I'm in the sixth arrondissement I step inside for a moment's quiet reflection. It is a peaceful counterweight to the constant action outside, and it reminds me of the reasons we sought out Bosgouet in the first place. Where Normandy has a bucolic stillness, Paris pulses.

I roamed the streets, the late autumn sun on my back and the hum of city life in my ears. Feeling like a true Parisian, I popped in to a few of the fabric stores hidden away in cobblestone lanes behind the boulevard. I sought out some fabric remnants that I planned to make into cushion covers and bought 5 metres of a Pierre Frey fabric that I thought would work beautifully on an old chair I wanted to re-upholster.

I made my way to the Café Marly and, not wanting to go against the indulgent feel of the afternoon, I ordered a flute of Billiecarte, which was served with a dish of salmon and chive blinis, wasabi peas and warm, pan-tossed walnuts – heaven!

Waiting for my dear friend, I thought about how my experiences had given me a stronger sense of myself. I had been gradually stripping away the extraneous things that I'd pinned to my life in Melbourne – all the unthinking routines and urban distractions. I was surprised by what was revealed underneath. Knowing what really mattered to me inspired a confidence I'd never felt before. I thought about how our children had become far more confident, too. I had such admiration for their diligence and perseverance in overcoming the frustrations of learning a new language to make new friends. To see a child branch out in a strange new world, despite the obvious constraints of language and culture, is the stuff that makes a parent's heart sing. I reflected that at Bosgouet each of us had found a new incarnation, a little bit of ourselves that we would not have known existed if we hadn't taken this opportunity.

I checked my watch; it was right on seven o'clock. Jacquie would be only moments away. I couldn't wait to find out what our night in Paris had in store for us.

Autumn

recipes

Scallops Brionne

This almost-effortless entrée always gets a great response from those around the table. For special occasions serve the scallops in their shells. Serves 6.

INGREDIENTS

125 g butter
1 kg scallops, roe on
50 ml Calvados
1 cup pouring cream
squeeze of lemon juice
sea salt and freshly ground
   black pepper

METHOD

Melt butter in a cast-iron frying pan, then sear scallops over high heat for 2 minutes on each side. Remove scallops and keep warm.

Deglaze pan with Calvados and cook until reduced by half. Add cream and a touch of lemon juice, then season to taste.

Stir until sauce thickens. Pour sauce over scallops and serve at once.

Watercress Soup

The fresh, peppery taste and vibrant colour of this traditional northern French recipe make it one of my favourites. Watercress is renowned as a spring-cleaning herb and is great for purifying the blood. Serves 6–8.

INGREDIENTS

60 g best Norman butter
1 large onion, chopped finely
2 celery stalks, chopped
1 leek, chopped finely, white
    part only
3 medium-sized potatoes (desiree
    or pontiac)
625 ml chicken stock
sea salt and freshly ground black
    pepper
625 ml full-cream milk
2 bunches watercress, chopped
    (I use the whole of the
    watercress, but the tough
    stalks can be removed)
crème fraîche and chopped chives,
    to serve

METHOD

Using a heavy-based saucepan, melt the butter over low heat. Add the onion, celery and leek and cook until they are softened and translucent. Add diced potatoes and a dash of stock to the saucepan, cover and cook for 10 minutes. Season onion, leek and potatoes with salt and pepper. Add milk and the rest of the stock, bring to the boil and then reduce heat and simmer for about 15 minutes or until potatoes are tender.

Stir in watercress and cook, uncovered, until watercress is just cooked, 3–4 minutes.

Purée soup with a hand-held blender until smooth. Add a little extra milk if the soup is too thick. Taste and add a little more salt and pepper if necessary. Serve chilled or piping hot topped with crème fraîche and chopped chives.

Soufflés Choux-fleurs

Soufflés are the perfect entrée – rich and warming and yet light enough not to spoil the next course. You could replace the Gruyère with blue cheese, if you prefer a stronger taste. Serves 6.

INGREDIENTS

butter, for greasing
¼ cup grated Parmesan, plus
    extra, for sprinkling
1 medium head cauliflower,
    florets separated
2 tablespoons lemon juice
125 g Philadelphia cream cheese
5 eggs, separated
¼ cup crème fraîche
¼ teaspoon sea salt
¼ teaspoon freshly ground
    white pepper
¼ teaspoon ground nutmeg
freshly chopped chives
2 tablespoons grated Gruyère

METHOD

Preheat oven to 190°C (270°F).

Butter 6 individual ½ cup soufflé dishes. Sprinkle finely grated Parmesan in the prepared soufflé dishes for an extra cheesy coating.

Drizzle the cauliflower florets with the lemon juice and steam for 4–5 minutes or until tender. Cool slightly. Purée with a hand-held blender.

In a medium-sized bowl, beat cream cheese with a hand-held electric beater until creamy. Beat in egg yolks one at a time, crème fraîche, salt, white pepper, nutmeg, chives and cheeses. Mix in the puréed cauliflower.

In a large bowl, beat egg-whites until peaks form; using a metal spoon, gently fold egg-whites into cauliflower mixture. Spoon mixture into buttered soufflé dishes and bake for 25 minutes or until risen and golden. Don't open the oven door to check on the soufflés' progress until you're certain they're done; no one likes deflated soufflés. Serve at once.

Milk-fed Veal with Girolles

This is a quintessentially French dish: rich, creamy, decadent. Every regional French bistro worth its salt has a version of this dish; it is often served with fresh tagliatelle. Serves 4.

INGREDIENTS

100 g unsalted butter
300 g mushrooms (a mixture of
   wild mushrooms, if you can find
   them – in France I like to use
   girolles), trimmed and wiped
   with a damp cloth
1 clove garlic, finely chopped
1 sprig thyme, leaves picked
⅔ cup pouring cream
4 x 150 g veal escalopes (also sold
   as veal schnitzel or medallions)
sea salt and freshly ground
   black pepper
¼ cup apple cider

METHOD

In a frying pan over high heat, melt half the butter until it starts to foam. Add mushrooms and coat them in butter. Reduce heat, cover pan and cook mushrooms for around 3 minutes or until lightly coloured. Add garlic and thyme and cook for another 5 minutes. Gently stir in cream and simmer for 5–7 minutes or until sauce has thickened.

Season veal lightly. Place another large frying pan over high heat and melt the rest of the butter until it turns a nutty brown. Add escalopes to the pan and cook for 3 minutes each side. Remove escalopes from pan and keep warm.

Deglaze the veal pan with apple cider, then bring to the boil over high heat, stirring to scrape up any brown bits from the bottom of the pan. Stir cider into the mushroom sauce.

Spoon sauce over the veal and serve.

Herbed Chicken

I'd often make this delicious, moist roast chook for our Sunday family lunch. The mustard and herbs give the dish an intoxicating smell as it cooks. Serves 4.

INGREDIENTS

2 teaspoons each of chopped
   flat-leaf parsley, sage,
   rosemary and thyme
½ teaspoon mustard powder
2 cloves garlic, finely chopped
½ teaspoon sea salt
½ teaspoon freshly ground
   black pepper
1 x 1.5 kg organic chicken
juice of 2 lemons
2 tablespoons olive oil

METHOD

Preheat oven to 180°C (350°F).

Combine herbs, mustard, garlic, sea salt and freshly ground black pepper in a small bowl and set aside.

Rinse chicken thoroughly, remove giblets, then pat dry with kitchen paper and place in a roasting pan. Rub half of the herb mixture inside the chicken and half of it outside the chicken. Combine lemon juice and olive oil in a small bowl, then drizzle over chicken.

Roast chicken for 90 minutes or until juices run clear when the thigh joint is pierced with a knife or skewer.

Serve with a selection of your favourite roast vegetables.

Chicken and Leek Pie

This pot pie is terrific comfort food: warming, heartening and perfect for dinner on a chilly night. Serves 8.

INGREDIENTS

30 g butter
4 chicken breast fillets, cut into
    bite-sized pieces
2 onions, finely chopped
1 clove garlic, crushed
450 ml chicken stock
sea salt and freshly ground
    black pepper
2 leeks, white part only,
    thinly sliced
⅔ cup double cream
squeeze of lemon juice
2 sheets frozen ready-made
    puff pastry, thawed
1 egg, lightly beaten

METHOD

Melt butter over low heat and gently cook chicken for 3–4 minutes, or until white; take care not to brown. Add onion and garlic and cook for another 5 minutes. Add stock, season to taste and bring to the boil over medium heat, then reduce heat to low and simmer gently for around 15 minutes or until chicken is tender.

Meanwhile, cook leeks in a saucepan of salted water for a few minutes until tender, then drain.

Add cream to chicken mixture, then bring to the boil over medium–high heat and simmer for about 6–8 minutes or until a thick sauce consistency. Season to taste and add a squeeze of lemon juice. Set the pie filling aside until it is cold.

Preheat oven to 200°C (400°F). Line a 25 cm pie dish with one of the pastry sheets. Combine the chicken mixture and leeks in the pastry shell. Place the remaining pastry sheet over the pie, trimming to fit the dish, then make a small slit in the centre. Glaze with beaten egg and bake for 40 minutes or until golden brown.

Serve immediately.

Normandy Apple Cake

It is difficult to conceive of cooking in Normandy without apples.
As well as being the key ingredient in the region's ubiquitous cider,
they are incorporated into almost any type of cooking and baking
you can imagine. A slice of this teacake is a perfect mid-afternoon
treat. Serves 8–10.

INGREDIENTS

4 granny smith apples, peeled,
  cored and roughly chopped
1 tablespoon brown sugar
250 g unsalted butter
1 cup caster (superfine) sugar
4 eggs
2 cups self-raising (self-rising) flour
1 cup milk
freshly grated nutmeg, to taste
pouring cream, to serve

METHOD

Preheat oven to 180°C (350°F).

Place apples, brown sugar and ½ cup water in
a saucepan, then cook over medium heat for
10 minutes or until apples are soft. Drain and
leave to cool.

Using hand-held electric beaters, cream butter and
sugar. Add eggs, one at a time, beating well after
adding each one. Sift in flour and slowly add milk,
beating to combine. Pour batter into a 28 cm cake
pan. Top with cooled stewed apples and sprinkle
with a little freshly grated nutmeg.

Bake cake for 50 minutes or until a skewer inserted
in the centre withdraws clean.

Serve warm or at room temperature with fresh cream.

Chocolate Tart

This mouth-watering chocolate tart should be served in smallish portions; its richness can bring even the most avid chocoholic unstuck. Serves 8–10.

INGREDIENTS

Chocolate Pastry
175 g unsalted butter, chopped
100 g icing sugar
1 egg yolk
250 g plain (all-purpose) flour
2 tablespoons Dutch-process cocoa powder
1–2 tablespoons iced water

Chocolate Filling
3 egg yolks
2 eggs
¼ cup caster (superfine) sugar
150 g butter
240 g dark couverture chocolate (at least 70 per cent cocoa solids)

METHOD

For pastry, pulse butter and icing sugar together in a food processor until pale and creamy. Add egg yolk and pulse to combine. Add sifted flour and cocoa and mix in, then add water; the dough will be moist. Wrap in plastic film, then chill in the refrigerator for 2 hours.

Preheat oven to 200°C (400°F). Lightly grease a 40 x 15 cm rectangular tart tin with a removable base (you could also use a 28 cm tart tin with a removable base). This dough can be quite tricky, so rather than rolling out with a rolling pin press it directly into the tin. Cover with plastic film and freeze for 1 hour.

Cover pastry base with baking paper and fill with pastry weights. Bake for 10 minutes, then remove pastry weights and baking paper and push the pastry back into the tin to keep its shape. Return to oven and cook for another 15–20 minutes or until golden and dry. Leave to cool.

Reduce oven temperature to 130°C (255°F). Meanwhile, for chocolate filling, beat egg yolks, eggs and sugar together with hand-held electric beaters.

Melt butter and chocolate in a microwave or a heatproof bowl placed over a saucepan of simmering water, then stir until smooth and leave to cool slightly. Gently fold chocolate mixture into egg mixture. Pour into pastry shell and bake for 15 minutes or until filling is set around the edge, but still a little wobbly in the middle. Leave to cool before serving.

Pear Tarte Tatin

This glazed upside-down pastry is traditionally made with apples, but I think the pears give the tart a lovely texture. Serves 6–8.

INGREDIENTS

⅓ cup soft brown sugar
35 g unsalted butter
1–2 firm pears, peeled, halved,
    cored, then each half cut into
    8 thin wedges
2 teaspoons freshly grated ginger
½ vanilla bean, split lengthwise,
    seeds scraped into small bowl
1 sheet frozen puff pastry, thawed
ice-cream, to serve

METHOD

Preheat oven to 190°C (375°F).

Melt sugar, butter and 1 tablespoon water in a heavy-based 20 cm non-stick ovenproof frying pan over low heat until sugar dissolves. Increase heat to high and boil for a few minutes or until syrup is dark amber, taking care not to burn. Remove from heat immediately and leave to cool so that bubbles subside. Toss pears with grated ginger and vanilla seeds, then arrange slices, overlapping, in a circle in the frying pan, placing a few around the edge, if necessary.

Cut puff pastry into a round slightly bigger than the frying pan. Place puff pastry round on top of pear mixture in frying pan, then tuck in edges around pears. Bake tart for about 35 minutes or until pastry is puffed and golden.

Invert tart onto a large plate and serve hot with ice-cream or at room temperature.

À table!

(dinner is served!)

*I*n winter the weeks seemed to move a bit slower, as if they were weighed down with the same sorts of heavy coats that we had to put on. Melbourne's wet, grey winters were insufficient training for these frozen northern ones; we had to buy whole wardrobes' worth of new jackets and thermals. The onset of winter meant that our menu was modified a bit, too. We moved on to hearty vegetable soups and warming savoury stews all eaten in front of a blazing fire.

To shrug off the cold-weather sluggishness I made sure to take regular constitutionals around the park or into the village. The crisp air was invigorating when I walked briskly and I was able to take in the park's wildlife, some of which still seemed odd to my Australian eyes. One morning I spied six deer grazing contentedly in the park, the winter sun shining down on their fluffy white derrières. Nearby there were three tiny red squirrels that scurried up and down a heavily laden walnut tree. As I wondered what the French word for 'squirrel' was, I saw three brooding figures off in the distance at the edge of the barren forest. They stood still with their guns slung over their shoulders, waiting patiently for *la chasse* (the hunt) to begin.

That afternoon, once the kids had come home from school, I convinced them to step back out into the cold to keep me company on a walk around one of Bosgouet's little forests. We headed across the park. I held the gloved hands of Millie and Alex, and Lachlan and Maddie followed close behind. The trees had all been denuded of their leaves and their branches stood out starkly against the quickly fading afternoon light. The floor of the forest cracked loudly beneath our feet, and the kids ran back and forth, collecting the prickly cases of fallen chestnuts. We roasted these over the embers of one of our fires that night and had the crunchy insides as an after-dinner treat. I stashed some away for a chestnut and mushroom terrine I'd been planning for dinner the next night.

Our constant flow of visitors had by this time become a trickle. We were grateful to be able to reclaim some family time. One Sunday, after a hearty breakfast of freshly baked croissants, we six decided to head off to Le Bec-Hellouin, a small village upstream on the Risle River. We had heard about

The Bosgouet village band.

ÉGLISE

a Sunday service at the Abbaye du Bec-Hellouin, a monastic abbey that dates back to the eleventh century. I confess that we were more interested in hearing the chanting of the white-robed monks than the sermon itself. The chanting resonates beautifully throughout the large abbey and the ringing of the church bells echoes across the Risle. We left the abbey feeling quite tranquil. Our next stops were the trash and treasure and fresh-food markets at Brionne. In wintertime the markets take on a different feel. They stock hand-painted ornaments for Christmas trees and small handicrafts for gifts. We left the markets saddled with one or two precious items, and hot chickens, *pommes de terre*, roasted pork hocks, fresh baguettes, Livarot and a creamy *citron* tart.

Out and about in Rouen

Bosgouet is only fifteen minutes away from the city of Rouen, the capital of Haute-Normandie (Upper Normandy). Geographically Rouen sits in north-west France between Paris and Le Havre. As in Paris, the Seine splits the city into a left and a right bank. A day trip to Rouen was one of our family's favourite excursions. We loved to wander through the maze of cobble-stone streets in the old city, located on the right bank, admiring the intricate stonework and the magnificent half-timbered houses. The kids said it's like a whole town made up of Diagon Alleys.

Each year in the weeks leading up to Christmas an enormous ice-skating rink is set up in front of Notre Dame Cathedral near the centre of the town.

White-robed monks at Bec-Hellouin.

The winter we were there the kids went wild for it. They'd spend countless hours whizzing around the rink, practising dare-devil jumps and other limb-threatening manoeuvres.

In medieval times Rouen was a significant and prosperous city and it has a rich – and bloody – history. In the course of the Hundred Years' War, waged between the British and the French, Rouen was captured by the English and held under their control for thirty years from 1419. In 1431 Joan of Arc was tried and executed as a heretic at the place du Vieux-Marché, the old marketplace.

Before her death, Joan was said to have plaintively cried out, 'Oh Rouen, art thou then my final resting place?' One can only assume that her complaint had more to do with her impending death than a prejudice against this lovely city. After her execution, Joan of Arc's ashes and miraculously unburned heart were thrown into the river Seine. She was canonised in 1920 and pronounced a patron saint of France.

These days the market square is a vibrant space filled with fruit and flower stalls. The brown-and-white half-timbered houses that border the south end of the square have been converted into street cafés. A modern memorial church dedicated to Joan sits in one corner of the square, and the actual site of Joan of Arc's barbecue, as the kids referred to it, is marked with an imposing 20-metre-high bronze cross.

Allied troops heavily bombed Nazi-occupied Rouen during the Second World War, killing many of the townspeople and destroying large parts of the city, including all its bridges and sections of its historical centre and industrial quarter. Huge amounts of the civic budget have been devoted to rebuilding the old city; much of the restoration has tried to recreate the city's medieval heritage, or at least a modernised conception of it. The tourist brochures

À table! 253

rather dryly proclaim modern-day Rouen, France's biggest river port, to be a hub of industry and commerce, but in my opinion this sells the city short. The townspeople, the Rouennais, are much more spirited than that. Rouen has a lively cultural scene and is a mecca for restaurant goers.

One of Rouen's most recognisable monuments is the Grosse Horloge (Great Clock), which adorns an archway spanning rue de Grosse-Horloge, a bustling pedestrian mall that connects the place du Vieux-Marché and the place de la Cathédrale. The astronomical clock is ornately decorated; its underside depicts John the Baptist as a shepherd tending to a flock of sheep. The single hand of the Grosse Horloge marks the hour, while other parts indicate the week and the current phase of the moon. The clock was built in 1389 and was originally housed in a belfry to one side of the arch. The eminently practical Rouennais complained that it sat too far above street level to be of any use. Quite sensibly it was moved to a lower position, on the arch, in 1527.

Victor Hugo dubbed Rouen 'the city of a hundred spires', and Rouen's churches are some of the most beautiful in France. A short walk east of the place du Vieux-Marché is the Cathédrale de Notre-Dame, a gothic cathedral built in the twelfth and thirteenth centuries. Claude Monet became preoccupied with how changing daylight affected the west façade of this cathedral. He painted this aspect over thirty times, most notably in the lambent morning light. The Chapelle de la Vierge in the cathedral holds the renaissance tombs of the cardinals d'Amboise, as well as the actual heart of Richard the Lionheart.

For the Webster family a typical day in Rouen started at our favourite eatery on rue de Grosse-Horloge, just underneath the street's famous namesake. The eatery's specialities are steaming mugs of hot chocolate so rich that they would constitute a meal on their own and croissants warm from

Images of Joan of Arc appear throughout the region.

Rouen's Grosse Horloge - the astronomical clock.

John the Baptist carved into the
archway under the Grosse Horloge.

the oven. The rustic melodies of street musicians generally accompanied breakfast. After we were sufficiently nourished, we headed off to wander the streets.

We learnt very early on that you have to book well in advance for Saturday or Sunday lunch in any of Rouen's best restaurants. We loved the old French atmosphere of La Bouffray, a small restaurant in a half-timbered house that dates back to the eleventh century, complete with polished beams and weighty French country-style interior. Madame and Monsieur, an elderly but spry couple, run La Bouffray without help. Madame is well known in Rouen for her dense flourless chocolate cake. The menu is limited to three or four choices at each course. The offerings are very traditional Norman fare but the menu changes constantly. We were always delighted with the meals that emerged from Madame's kitchen. One of our favourite meals at La Bouffray was a filleted Saint Pierre served with a *beurre blanc* sauce infused with tomato and saffron.

Another of my Rouennais favourites was Restaurant Gill, a modern two-Michelin-star establishment sitting on the banks of the Seine. The chef, Gilles Tournadre, has an innovative and creative menu, using the best Norman produce. His *pigeon à la rouennais* (pigeon in puff pastry) will have you dreaming about returning to Rouen. At Restaurant Gill we often had the *menu dégustation*, eight little elegantly presented courses of superbly balanced flavours. One of the first meals I experienced at Gill was pan-fried goose foie gras drizzled in a chocolate sauce. The chilled foie gras melts away as soon as it hits your tongue; goose foie gras has a silken texture more subtle in flavour than duck liver, and was wonderfully offset by the slightly bitter chocolate sauce. I can still recall the exact sensation of eating the dish. It had me counting down the days until our next booking.

Christmas markets outside the Rouen cathedral.

Our children were always welcome at Gill and were offered new and interesting dishes that they would have never come across were they not living in this corner of the world. Gill's two Michelin stars mean that a dinner or a lunch there was reserved for special occasions. However, at least once a month we seemed to have yet another visitor staying with us keen to experience somewhere very special. We were happy to oblige . . . Lucky us!

Back in Bosgouet, as I tramped through the wintry woods on another of my afternoon walks, my thoughts shifted to Melbourne, where we'd be returning in only a few short months' time. I reflected that at Bosgouet the sense of simplicity and relaxation we all experienced was in part related to responding to life's rhythms. I always visited farmers' markets in Australia and I bought as much of my family's food from local sources as I was able to, but this was a difficult exercise. I'd love to be like one of those legendary French housewives who go out to buy fresh produce every day. In France eating locally produced food is ingrained in the culture of every village. Here, supermarkets are an absolute last resort. I admire the slow, methodical pace of French market shopping – taking the time to talk with those who produce the food you eat – and the approach of buying little amounts often. The harsh chemicals that are used in Australia to preserve fruit and vegetables long enough to get to the supermarket are not as common here. The shelf-life of produce is shorter but the taste is incomparable.

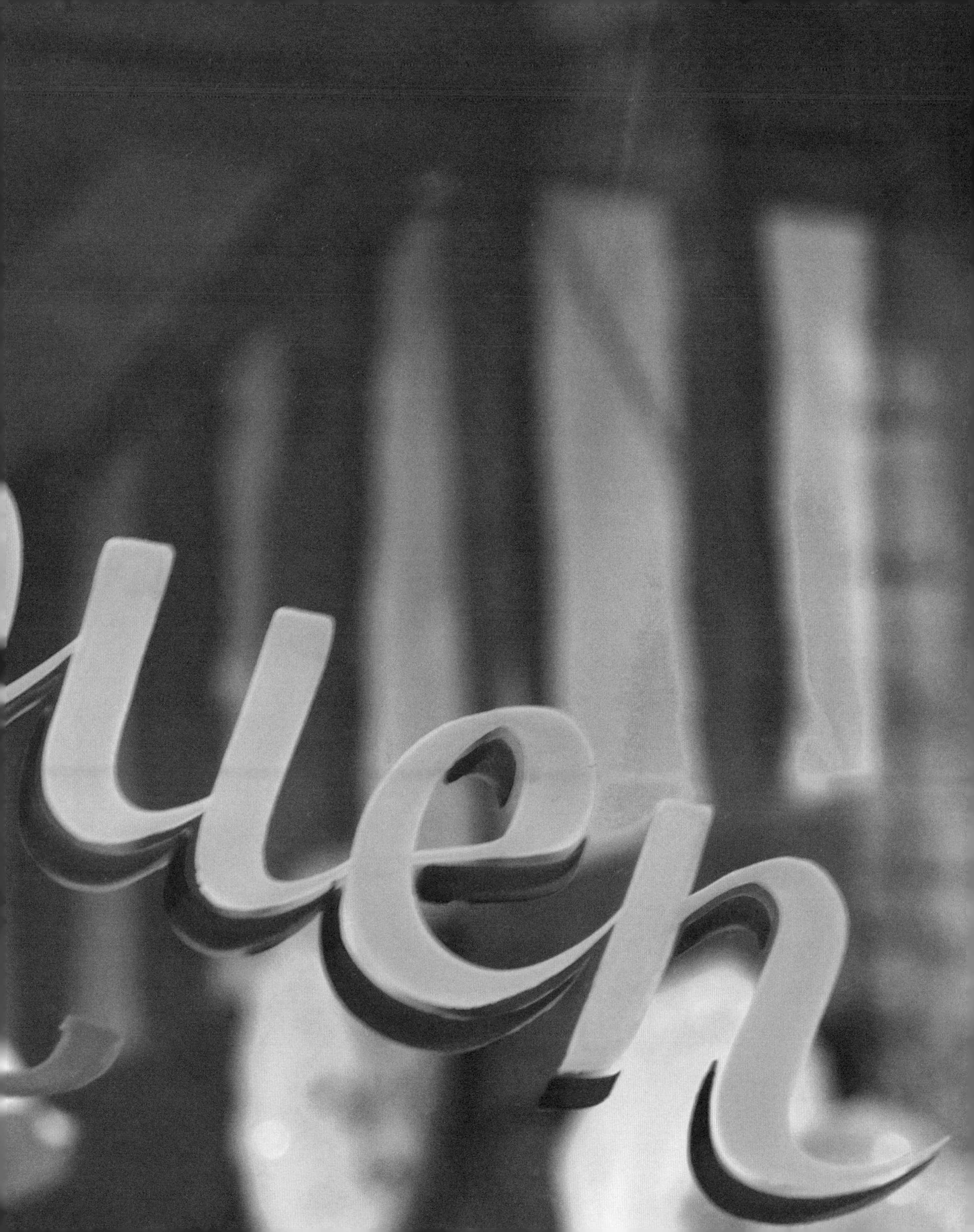
uen

As I sit here and write I can't help but think that if we all made little changes toward buying local produce, it could only be for the good of the planet and the good of ourselves.

For the time we lived at Bosgouet we did not watch television, apart from the occasional movie on DVD. We just didn't want commercial television clogging our lives the way it had in Australia. The kids were horrified when we first told them about this idea, but they quickly got used to it. Instead we listened to French radio, which was extremely good for our language skills, and we played boardgames the way I remember doing as a child. We took long walks together and sat around talking for hours. We had some great friends from Australia come to stay with us for three months with their two children, and most nights ended with a competitive game of cards and many laughs. The parade of friends and family passing through Bosgouet was far from the chore that it could have been – it was quite the opposite, in fact. We enjoyed the chance to get to know people so much better than at the occasional dinner

at an over-crowded, noisy restaurant. The new friendships we had made at Bosgouet – with our neighbours and fellow villagers – had been unexpected, and these were one of the greatest joys of our time in France.

The challenge of course would be to take all that Bosgouet and France had taught us and bring a little of it back to Australia – just as we had brought a little of Australia to *le petit village* of Bosgouet. All the children of the village now spoke some English and were immensely proud of their achievements. My proudest moment was when they sang 'Give Me a Home Among the Gumtrees' in rural French accents. The exchange of cultures between the residents of Bosgouet and our family had been great, and I thought the small changes were likely to stay – besides, we would be back each year!

Joyeux Noël

To mark the countdown to Christmas we hold our traditional Webster tree trimming early each December. That winter we hauled in a 15-foot beauty cut from a huge pine in our own forest. We drank egg nog and trimmed the tree together as a family, while Christmas music blared throughout the house. The tree trimming isn't about getting the tree to look like it's out of a glossy magazine, but more about rediscovering the precious ornaments that have been made by the children over the years, or collected on one of our trips. I loved listening to the kids as they reminisced.

'I made this one in kindergarten!'

'Oh, this is one of Johnny and Sarah's!'

'I forgot that we bought these angels at the Raspail market in Paris.'

The festivities at Bosgouet started earlier than usual with the arrival of a houseful of some of our dearest friends a few days before Christmas. We celebrated with a group of twenty-four – twelve children and twelve adults – the perfect number to ensure some serious revelry. With such a large crowd all trying to do everything at once, it was necessary to impose some order. Every member of the household was delegated tasks to ensure the preparations took place without too many complications. There was always another pot of coffee to be made or a dishwasher to be unloaded. The chatter was constant and everyone mucked in to keep the house running as smoothly as possible.

The first job was to create a Christmas wreath to hang on the château's door. I had seen a beautiful example when visiting New York a while back and I was determined to make a replica for Bosgouet. The wreath wasn't traditionally Christmasy – I used dried hydrangeas and offcuts of evergreens instead of spiky fir branches to give it a more subtly festive feel. The kids

hung it on the front door of the château and invited the adults to attend an unveiling ceremony. They sang Christmas carols as they excitedly pulled the adults by their hands out onto the stone steps. The kids all performed drum rolls on their thighs before Maddie removed the blanket covering the wreath with a flourish. *Voilà!* The wreath looked magnificent!

We began to think about decorations for the dining room table, and it was the kids' idea to make Christmas boxes to be laid at each guest's place. Inside these hand-folded boxes was a tiny wooden angel that could be pinned like a brooch, and a Christmas joke that the children had great fun writing themselves – I could hear their raucous laughter from the other end of the house! We tied the boxes with fine red satin ribbon, finished off with fresh holly from our forest.

Given how different our surroundings were to our usual Christmas celebrations, we thought that we should develop a few new traditions. We made the table centrepiece ourselves, using only what we could find on the forest floor – with so much natural beauty just outside we would have been mad to use something store-bought. All the guests were sent out to gather pine cones, holly and other evergreens for the display. While they were outside, my good friend and right-hand woman in the kitchen, Patricia, a chef from Canada, started to make a gingerbread château, complete with sugar figurines of all the children. Once the kids got back from their treasure hunt, Patricia taught them how to make gingerbread houses of their own. This was a great project for all the kids, who, not limited by stuffy unimaginative adult brains, created not only gingerbread houses, but gingerbread castles, teepees and ski-lodges, too. We also whipped up shortbread, chocolate truffles, traditional mince tarts and lemon cordial.

Feeding so many mouths over the holiday season was a bit of a challenge. I stuck to good food that I knew wouldn't cause me to tear my hair out while I was preparing it. I loved that peaceful time before the hordes woke up and came hunting for their first meal of the day – luckily I'm an early riser. Energised by a strong cup of tea, I would mix up a batch of muffins, and then it would be off to the local *boulangerie* for fresh croissants and bread. One morning Madame smiled warmly and enquired about how many guests we had for Christmas. Her eyes opened wide when I told her the number of people we had staying with us. I ordered four-dozen croissants, cleaning her out completely until her husband could manage to get another batch from out of his wood-fired oven. Breakfast was never typically French at Bosgouet as I always offered bacon and eggs as well as fruit, yoghurt and fresh pastries. We ate breakfast in the basement kitchen, which was toasty warm because of the extra heat generated from the mammoth Rosières cooker.

One thing was certain, when people came to stay at Bosgouet their appetites increased dramatically – horse riding, bike riding and long country walks all made for hungry guests. Making sure that no one's stomach was rumbling was a full-time job. It often seemed as if we'd only just cleaned up from breakfast when a few of the kids would appear at the kitchen door, drawing semi-circles with their pointed toes and looking wistfully at the fridge.

Our village church.

On Christmas Eve the entire household attended mass in the local village church for a special children's service. The nativity was played out while hundreds of candles twinkled. Music resonated through the church. There is a tradition at this service for the tiniest baby in the village to be bought in by their parents and placed in a manger. Sometimes a donkey is also paraded through the church up to the manger, but I'm guessing this depends on availability – that year we were *sans* donkey much to our kids' disappointment.

'*Ah! Quel Grand Mystère*' (Ah! What a mystery) is a traditional French Christmas carol from the nineteenth century. As far as I know, there is no equivalent English version. Our kids had learnt this carol at school and took great delight in teaching it to all the other children who had come to Bosgouet for Christmas. All the parents were touched when, to our surprise, we heard the children chiming in with the chorus of voices at the church.

Although these days attendance for mass on Christmas Eve is down, it is still an important part of Noël for many French families. We never attend midnight mass in Australia, but somehow in France it seems the right thing to do. The mass is traditionally followed by a huge feast, called le Réveillon. *Réveillon* comes from the verb *réveiller*, to wake up or revive, and the ritual is used to symbolically awaken oneself to the meaning of Jesus' birth. It is typically French to seek enlightenment through food. We decided to have our Réveillon at the château. We returned to Bosgouet after mass to a spread of roast pork, coq au vin, saffron risotto, salads, vegetables and a huge array of cheeses and desserts. I wondered how we would find room for all the food the next day.

As part of Réveillon, it's customary to leave a candle burning in case the Virgin Mary passes by. We set up huge hurricane lanterns and had them on each windowsill of the reception floor of the château, where they burned all night long.

On Christmas Eve, after Réveillon, we encouraged all the children staying at Bosgouet to do as the French children did: put their shoes in front of the fireplace, in the hope that Père Noël would fill them with gifts. We reminded

the kids about Père Fouettard, who gives out spankings to bad children. The French obviously prefer something more hard-line to Santa Claus's benign coal-giving form of castigation. Having assured the kids that Père Fouettard's spanking rampage was not going to affect any of them, it was *bonne nuit* to all, and the weary revellers took to their beds.

Christmas morning began with steaming hot mugs of coffee, egg nog, large platters of egg-and-bacon toasted baguettes, warm croissants and *pain au chocolat* around the twinkling Christmas tree. Pyjama-clad adults found comfy spots on the sofas in front of the fire. The fire was not nearly as warm as the giant furnace that powers the château's hydronic heating system, but then again, the furnace was not nearly so pretty. As children eagerly foraged through the gifts left in their shoes, paper flew all over the room and the squeals of delight echoed through every room and corridor of the château. Presents unwrapped, the kids played with their new gadgets while the adults took a walk to build up their appetites for Christmas lunch.

I had spent a lot of time deciding what would go on our Christmas menu; it had to be just right. In the end I went with an entrée of lobster bisque, followed by turkey with cranberry stuffing, roast duck with pomegranate and chestnut purée, potatoes dauphines, tomatoes with sage and onion stuffing and a baked leg of ham. It all went down a treat, but the *Bûche Noëlle* I served for dessert got the most adulation. Christmas lunches in France stretch out over four or five hours — just as well considering the amount of food.

After lunch the children treated us to a play that they had been rehearsing, which was aptly titled 'The True Meaning of Christmas'. They had raided our wardrobes for costumes and had hand-drawn signs which were used to cue laughter, gasps of horror and applause from the audience. Père Fouettard – looking like a pantomime villain: moustachioed and cape-clad – made a surprise appearance, threatening spankings for all. Thankfully he was easily chased off by the hero of the day, Père Noël, and we all learned a valuable lesson about the real meaning of Christmas. The play ended with a reprise of '*Ah! Quel Grand Mystère*', and our little thespians received thunderous applause.

In France mistletoe is hung above the door during the Christmas season to bring good fortune throughout the next year. We put a sprig over a doorway in the *salle à manger* and each set of parents lined up to kiss underneath it. The kids, of course, shrieked the whole time.

As Pete and I kissed under the mistletoe, I thought how lucky I was.

Winter
recipes

Classic French Onion Soup

Rustic and hearty, this soup could really stand up as a meal on its own.
It's all the better if accompanied by a fine glass of Bordeaux. Serves 4.

INGREDIENTS

750 g brown onions, thinly sliced
750 g red onions, thinly sliced
4 cloves garlic
100 g butter
50 g flour
3 litres good beef stock
500 ml Bordeaux
2 bay leaves
4 sprigs thyme
1 baguette
100 g Parmesan and Gruyère,
  grated
truffle salt

METHOD

Over low heat sauté onions and garlic in butter until soft and caramelised. This process will take 20–25 minutes. Stir in the flour and simmer for 3 minutes until the onion mixture thickens.

Add the stock, wine, bay leaves and thyme. Bring the soup to a boil and then simmer gently for 1 hour.

This soup is even better if made one day in advance to allow all the flavours to develop. To serve, ladle soup into soup bowls and top with toasted baguette. Sprinkle with Parmesan and Gruyère and a little truffle salt. Place under a hot grill for 10 minutes or until the cheese is bubbling and browned.

Celeriac and Parsnip Gratin

Madame Flamant, one of our neighbours, gave me a version of this recipe one day as we chatted in her living room, watching as a wild Norman storm raged outside. Against my protestations, she braved the deluge to duck out to her potager to get a couple of parsnips for me to take home. Serves 6–8.

INGREDIENTS

1 celeriac, peeled, halved lengthwise and thinly sliced
2 parsnips, thinly sliced
4 potatoes, thinly sliced
1 cup pouring cream
100 ml milk
1 clove garlic, crushed
Parmesan, for grating
½ cup breadcrumbs made from day-old bread

METHOD

Preheat oven to 180°C (360°F).

Place alternate layers of sliced celeriac, parsnip and potato into a 1 litre-capacity baking dish.

Heat cream and milk with garlic in a small saucepan over medium heat and pour over to cover the vegetables and fill the dish. Top with some freshly grated Parmesan and the breadcrumbs.

Cover with foil and bake for at least 90 minutes. Uncover for the final 30 minutes so the top can bubble and brown.

Roast Loin of Pork Stuffed with Apricots and Rosemary

I love the concentrated sweetness of dried fruit when combined with pork.
I sometimes replace the apricots in this dish with dried figs or prunes.
Serves 6.

INGREDIENTS

12 dried apricots
1.5 kg boneless pork loin roast,
    skin scored
sea salt and freshly ground black
    pepper
2 cloves garlic, cut into slivers
1 small piece (2 cm)
    chopped ginger
2 freshly picked sprigs rosemary
2 tablespoons olive oil
2 large red onions, quartered

Gravy
1 cup red wine
1 cup chicken stock
1 tablespoon red-wine vinegar
2 teaspoons cornflour (optional)

METHOD

Preheat oven to 180°C (360°F).

To avoid the pork's stuffing being too chewy, plump
up your apricots by letting them stand in a bowl of
boiling water for half an hour before you use them.

Place pork loin fat-side down. Leaving a 3 cm border
at each end, cut pork lengthwise to create a long
pouch. Drain and pat dry the apricots, then line the
pork cavity with them. Season the inside of the pouch.

Insert slivers of garlic and ginger and small sprigs
of rosemary into the slits in the pork skin. Rub pork
with olive oil and sea salt. Tie the loin together with
kitchen string at 5 cm intervals. Transfer pork to a
roasting pan. Pop onions around the edge of the pork
for roasting. Roast pork for 2 hours, then remove from
oven and leave to stand for 15 minutes.

Make the gravy by spooning off most of the fat from
the pan juices, then scrape the sides and base of the
roasting pan to release all the caramelised bits. Add
the wine and chicken stock to the pan and transfer
the pan to the stove top. Simmer on medium–low
heat until lightly thickened. If you prefer thicker gravy,
whisk cornflour with a little water and stir the mixture
into the juices. Swirl in a dash of red-wine vinegar
and you're all set.

Annik's Game Bourguignon

Annik regularly invites our entire family to her château at La Chouque. Her meals are hearty and provincial, and often include wild boar or venison. This slow-cooked, tender stew is perfect for a cold winter's night. Serves 4.

INGREDIENTS

olive oil, for cooking
12 rashers (slices) bacon,
    roughly chopped
2 large onions, sliced
1 kg venison, trimmed and cut
    into 4 cm pieces
sea salt and freshly ground
    black pepper
2 large carrots, sliced
1 x 750 ml bottle red wine
2 cups beef stock
1 x 400 g can chopped
    Italian tomatoes
1 bouquet garni (wrap up 8
    flat-leaf parsley sprigs, 1 large
    fresh bay leaf, 1 teaspoon dried
    thyme, 2 whole cloves or allspice
    berries and 3 large cloves
    crushed garlic in cheesecloth or
    muslin)
24 golden shallots, peeled
400 g button mushrooms, trimmed
1 sheet frozen ready-made puff
    pastry, thawed
1 egg, beaten

Beurre Manié
¼ cup plain (all-purpose) flour
2 tablespoons butter

METHOD

Heat a little of the oil over medium heat in a large frying pan. Sauté bacon to brown slightly, then set aside. Sauté onions in the same pan for 4–5 minutes or until brown, then remove and set aside. Working in batches, brown venison pieces on all sides in the bacon fat and oil over high heat, then season to taste. Transfer venison to a cast-iron casserole dish, along with bacon and onions.

Remove all but a little fat from the frying pan, then add carrots and brown them over medium heat. Add to the meat. Deglaze frying pan with 2–3 tablespoons of wine, pouring it and remaining wine into the casserole along with enough stock to almost cover the meat. Stir in chopped tomatoes and add bouquet garni. Bring this to a simmer over medium heat, then cover and simmer slowly over the lowest heat possible, either on the stove or in a preheated 150°C (300°F) oven, until meat is tender. I usually cook this for 2–3 hours.

To make the *beurre manié*, combine the flour and butter into a paste and set aside. ⟶

Sauté golden shallots and mushrooms in a little more oil in a frying pan over low heat until browned and just done. Set aside.

Drain meat and vegetables through a colander placed over a large saucepan, reserving sauce in a saucepan. Return venison to casserole dish and set aside. Press juices from the residue in the colander into the sauce. Boil sauce over high heat until reduced to 3 cups. Remove from heat, then whisk in the *beurre manié*. Place over medium heat, then simmer for 2 minutes to give sauce time to thicken slightly. Taste for seasoning and pour over the meat, stirring in the shallots and mushrooms.

Preheat oven to 180°C (350°F).

Top the casserole dish with a round of puff pastry, trimming it to fit, then make a small slit in the centre. Glaze with a beaten egg and bake for 20 minutes or until golden.

Serve immediately.

Mushroom and Chestnut Terrine

I like to try to find as many ways of using chestnuts as I can to make the most of their brief season. Here, I have added them to my interpretation of Canadian chef Christine Cushing's Wild Mushroom Terrine. Serves 6–8.

INGREDIENTS

½ cup dried porcini mushrooms
60 g butter
200 g mixed wild mushrooms, trimmed and finely chopped
8 chanterelle mushrooms
2 cloves garlic, chopped
sea salt and freshly ground black pepper
350 g pork mince
100 g duck mince
2 egg-whites
1 cup pouring cream
8 morel mushrooms
2 tablespoons chopped thyme
1 tablespoon chopped chives
1 cup freshly prepared chestnut purée or tinned equivalent
14 rashers bacon

METHOD

Preheat oven to 180°C (350°F).

Soak porcini mushrooms in boiling water for around 30 minutes. Drain mushrooms, gently squeezing out excess liquid. Finely slice them, then set aside.

Heat 2 tablespoons butter in a large frying pan over medium–high heat and gently sauté the diced wild mushrooms until tender; this should take around 4 minutes. Remove mushrooms from the pan, leaving the juices. Cook mushroom juices over low heat. In a few minutes the juices will reduce to a thick, syrupy consistency; remove from saucepan and set aside.

Put remaining butter in the same pan and, over high heat, sear the chanterelles whole with the garlic for 2–3 minutes. Season and set aside.

Mix together pork and duck mince with ½ teaspoon salt and gently incorporate egg-whites. Gradually add cream to mixture.

Remove morels' stalks and fill each cap with a few teaspoons of mince. Set aside. Fold mushroom glaze, herbs, porcini and wild mushrooms into remaining mince. Add chestnut purée and season. ⟶

Line a terrine 30 x 15 cm with 8 of the bacon slices across the width of the mould so the bacon hangs over the edge. Lay remaining bacon across the length of the mould, with 2 slices along the bottom of the mould and then 2 strips of bacon at either end so they hang over the top and bottom edges. There should be enough overhang to fold over and cover the top of the terrine once it is filled with mince.

Spread half the mince into the bacon-lined terrine mould, place the seared whole chanterelles and stuffed morels across the top of the mince. Spread the remaining mince over the mushrooms.

Fold the overhanging bacon strips to cover the top of the terrine. Then fold in the overhanging strips of bacon at either end to enclose the top of the terrine.

Put terrine mould in a baking dish. Fill baking dish with hot water to halfway up the sides of the mould to create a water bath. Bake in the oven for 75–90 minutes or until cooked through. Remove mould from water bath and leave to cool. Invert cooled terrine onto a platter.

Slice and serve. Serve with cornichons and mustard with a green salad. This will keep covered and refrigerated for up to a week.

Bûche Noëlle

This Christmas roll can be made one of two ways: either with a rich butter cream icing or simply filled with cream and berries and topped with a chocolate sauce. Serves 6–8.

INGREDIENTS

vegetable oil, for brushing
150 g caster (superfine) sugar
6 large free-range eggs, separated
250 g dark couverture chocolate
4 tablespoons self-raising flour

Cream Filling
400 ml double cream,
  lightly whipped
250 g raspberries
Drambuie, for drizzling
icing sugar, for dusting

Chocolate Sauce
100 g dark couverture chocolate
300 ml pouring cream

METHOD

Preheat oven to 220°C (450°F). Line a 23 x 33 cm / 9 x 13 cm Swiss roll pan with baking paper and brush lightly with oil.

Combine caster sugar and egg yolks in a bowl and whisk them together with hand-held electric beaters until light and fluffy. Melt chocolate with ⅓ cup cold water in a heatproof bowl over a saucepan of very gently simmering water, taking care that the base of the bowl doesn't touch the water. When chocolate has melted and is smooth, stir in sugar and egg mixture and the flour.

Meanwhile, whisk egg-whites with clean hand-held electric beaters until stiff but not dry. Gently fold a spoonful of the egg-whites into chocolate mixture to lighten it, then fold in remaining egg-whites. Pour batter gently into prepared pan and bake for 12–14 minutes or until risen and just firm to the touch. Transfer pan to a wire rack and leave to cool in the pan for at least 2 hours.

Once cold, lay a sheet of baking paper on a chopping board. Turn the whole cake onto the sheet of paper, with one swift movement, then remove pan. Carefully peel away the paper and trim edges to make them even. $\longrightarrow$

To assemble the cream filling, spread inverted cake with the whipped cream, scatter over the berries and add a few dribbles of Drambuie, if you like. Roll cake up as you would a Swiss roll; starting at the long side opposite you, use the baking paper to roll the cake towards you, encasing the cream and raspberry filling. Transfer to a flat serving dish.

For the sauce, very gently melt chocolate into the cream in a saucepan over low heat. Pour sauce over bûche just before serving.

Variation: Butter Cream Filling and Icing

For a richer version, beat 250 g softened unsalted butter until soft with hand-held electric beaters, then sift in 450 g icing sugar and 50 g cocoa powder. Add 2 tablespoons milk and combine together until soft. Spread half the icing over the cake, up to the edge. Roll cake up as you would a Swiss roll; starting at the long side opposite you, use the paper to roll cake towards you, around the icing. Transfer to a flat serving dish. Carefully spread remaining icing over the cake. Chill until needed, then decorate with festive decorations and sift over some icing sugar.

Galette du Roi

This French Christmas dessert is a delicious frangipane pastry. It has some wonderful traditions attached to it (see page 295). Serves 6–8.

INGREDIENTS

¼ cup almond paste (sold
   as marzipan)
¼ cup caster (superfine) sugar
60 g unsalted butter, softened,
   plus extra, for greasing
pinch of salt
2 eggs
¼ teaspoon vanilla extract
¼ teaspoon almond extract
⅓ cup plain (all-purpose) flour,
   plus extra for dusting
2 frozen puff pastry sheets, thawed
1 tiny china figurine
icing sugar, for dusting

METHOD

Purée almond paste, sugar, butter and salt in a food processor until smooth. Add 1 of the eggs and vanilla and almond extract and continue processing until incorporated. Add flour and pulse to mix it in. Set aside.

Invert a 22 cm pie plate onto one of the thawed pastry sheets and cut out a pastry round the size of the pie plate with the tip of a paring knife. Dust flour over base of the round and place it on a baking paper-lined tray. Chill in the refrigerator. Repeat with second sheet of puff pastry, then place on a lightly floured bench.

Beat remaining egg and brush some of it on top of second pastry round. Score decoratively all over the top, using the tip of a paring knife, but taking care not to cut all the way through, then make several small slits all the way through the pastry to create steam vents.

Place an oven rack in the bottom third of the oven, then preheat to 180°C (350°F). ⟶

Remove first pastry round from the refrigerator and brush some of the beaten egg in a 2 cm border around the edge. Mound the almond cream mixture in the centre, spreading slightly. Bury the figurine in the almond cream. Place the second pastry round on top and press the edges together.

Bake the galette for 13–15 minutes or until puffed and golden. Remove from oven and dust with icing sugar.

Place oven rack in the upper third of the oven and return galette to cook for another 12–15 minutes or until the edge is a deep golden brown. Transfer to a wire rack to cool slightly.

Galette du Roi

In France the tradition of serving this frangipane-filled tart can be traced back to the fourteenth century. La Galette du Roi *is served on 6 January, Epiphany, to commemorate the arrival of the three wise men visiting Jesus in his manger. A small bean, coin or porcelain figurine is baked inside the cake.*

Tradition also dictates that the cake be cut into as many slices as there are people present, plus one extra. The extra piece is called either la part du Bon Dieu *(God's piece),* la part de la Vierge *(the Virgin Mary's piece) or* la part du pauvre *(poor man's piece) and it is given to the first poor person who stops at the home.*

The youngest child is asked to go under the table while an adult cuts the galette into the number of serves required. As each slice is placed on a plate, the youngest child calls out from under the table who gets which slice. The person who discovers the figurine in their slice is designated king or queen for the day and gets to wear a golden crown.

Enfin

(at last)

I've come back to Bosgouet ahead of the family, for the summer, and now here it is: the first day of The French Table. I am almost electric with anticipation as I board the train at Gare de Rouen to travel to Paris to meet my first group: eleven eager Australians hailing from all over the country. I have a full week planned. Marieke Brugman will run the gourmet cooking classes; in the first class Marieke will teach the guests how to prepare a demitasse of pea and coriander, rabbit confit and a prune and Armagnac soufflé. At night I'll give the guests a taste of French home-style cuisine. I've also planned daytrips to Etretat, Honfleur, Deauville and Rouen. There, we'll visit the local markets and *foires à tout*; I'll also take my band of adventurers to see Monet's garden in Giverny. My lofty business idea is finally about to come to fruition — I feel extremely gratified on the one hand, and stomach-wrenchingly terrified on the other. I have put so much energy into the planning, what will I do if it doesn't come off?

We had arranged to meet at Gare Saint Lazare, under the famous old clock. But to my horror I realise that there are in fact two famous old clocks at the station. Cursing myself for not checking this beforehand, I dash from one clock to the other, trying to spot someone — anyone — who looks like they might be waiting for me. I have that small moment of panic that every host knows: no one is coming! What will I do? I finally catch a glimpse of a fellow standing amid a crowd, who looks as lost as I feel.

'Are you waiting for Jane?' I ask hesistantly.

'Yes!' comes the reply from all around the fellow; eleven friendly faces beam at me.

I happily introduce myself to everyone and do a quick head-count. Once we have made sure that we aren't missing any stragglers, it is all aboard for Rouen and then on to Bosgouet in a hired minibus. As we make our way through the Fôret de la Londe and turn the corner into the village of Bosgouet, the red and white of the château comes into view. The excited chatter of my guests gives way to little gasps — my heart beats a little louder with pride; this is my corner of Normandy!

We pull up to the château steps just minutes later, and I lead the group forward through the entrée and into one of the salons. I run through some housekeeping while they sip on tea and coffee and munch on orange cake.

After showing the guests to their rooms and letting them know that aperitifs will be served at 6.30 p.m., I run to the basement kitchen for last-minute preparations for the evening's meal. Everything is in place. My guests will try out my foie gras recipe as taught to me by Frederik all those months ago. For the main course I'll serve a dish with typical Norman flavours, just to help my visitors to acclimatise: pork fillet with bay leaves and fennel salt, wrapped in prosciutto and served with a sauce of apple cider and crème fraîche.

After dinner, our new friends are sated and happy, and head upstairs to retire for the night. Some of them promise to be Marieke's participants for yoga the next morning, while others say they'll accompany me for the 5-kilometre walk I like to do around the farmland of Bosgouet. As the last set of legs disappears up the staircase I let out a deep sigh. It feels like I've been holding my breath for years. I dash down to the belly of the château to run over the next day's itinerary with Marieke over a mug of herbal tea.

It is all going to work!

Address book

A few of my favourite places.

Restaurants, cafés, bars

Bourg-Achard

L'Amandier
581 route de Rouen
27310 Bourg-Achard
+33 2 32 57 11 49

Honfleur

Ferme Saint-Simeon
Rue Adolphe-Marais
14600 Honfleur
+33 2 31 81 78 00

Jazz Melody Piano Bar
58 rue Haute
14600 Honfleur
+33 2 31 89 36 24

La Fleur de Sel
17 rue Haute
14600 Honfleur
+33 2 31 89 01 92

La Terrasse et l'Assiette
8 place Sainte-Catherine
14600 Honfleur
+33 2 31 89 31 33

Sa Qua Na
22 place Hamelin
14600 Honfleur
+33 2 31 89 40 80

La Bouille

De la Poste
6 place du Bateau
76530 La Bouille
+33 2 35 18 03 90

Le Saint-Pierre
4 place du Bateau
76530 La Bouille
+33 2 32 68 02 01
www.restaurantlesaintpierre.com

Les Gastronomes
1 place du Bateau
76530 La Bouille
+33 2 35 18 02 07

Paris

Brasserie Lipp
51 boulevard Saint-Germain
75006 Paris
+33 1 45 48 53 91

Cafe Marly
Musee Du Louvre
93 rue de Rivoli
75001 Paris
+33 1 49 26 06 60

La Coupole
102 boulevard du Montparnasse
75014 Paris
+33 1 43 20 14 20

Les Deux Magots
6 place Saint-Germain des Prés
75006 Paris
+33 1 45 48 55 25

Rouen

Dame Cakes
70 rue Saint-Romain
76000 Rouen
+33 2 35 07 49 31

Gill
9 quai de la Bourse
76000 Rouen
+33 2 35 71 16 14
www.gill.fr

La Couronne
31 place du Vieux-Marché
76000 Rouen
+33 2 35 71 40 10
www.lacouronne.com.fr

Les Nymphéas
9 rue de la Pie
76000 Rouen
+33 2 35 89 26 69
www.les-nympheas.fr

Antiques

Deauville

Windsor Antiquités
5 place François André
14800 Deauville
+33 2 31 88 21 19

Elbeuf

Hôtel des Ventes de la Seine
85 rue des Martyrs
76500 Elbeuf
+33 2 35 33 28 96

Paris

Hôtel Drouot Paris
9 rue Drouot
75009 Paris
+33 1 42 73 36 74

Bookstores

Deauville

Librairie du Marché
Place du Marché
14800 Deauville
+33 2 31 88 92 95

Paris

Shakespeare and Company
37 rue de la Bucherie
75005 Paris
+33 1 43 26 96 50

Village Voice
Rue de Princesse
75006 Paris
+33 1 46 33 36 47

Museums, abbeys and gardens

Bayeux

Musee de la Tapisserie de Bayeux
Centre Guillaume-le-Conquerant
13 rue de Nesmond
14402 Bayeux
+33 2 31 51 25 50

Bec Hellouin

Abbaye du Bec-Hellouin
27800 Le Bec Hellouin
+33 2 32 43 72 60

Caen

Le Mémorial de Caen
Esplanade Général Eisenhower
14066 Caen
+33 2 31 06 06 44

Giverny

Jardin de Monet
84 rue Claude Monet
27620 Giverny
+33 2 32 51 28 21

Musee d'art Americain
99 rue Claude Monet
27620 Giverny
+33 2 32 51 94 65

Honfleur

Musee Eugene Boudin
Place Erik Satie
14600 Honfleur
+33 2 31 89 54 00

Paris

Musee de Orsay
62 rue de Lille
75007 Paris
+33 1 40 49 48 14

Rouen

Cathédrale Notre Dame de Rouen
Place de la Cathédrale
76000 Rouen
+33 2 35 71 85 65

Jardin des Plantes
114 ter avenue des Martyrs
    de la Résistance
76100 Rouen
+33 2 32 18 21 30

Musee des Beaux-Arts
Esplanade Marcel-Duchamp
76000 Rouen
+33 2 35 71 28 40

Palais de Justice
36 rue aux Juifs
76037 Rouen
+33 2 35 52 87 52

Hotels

Bec Hellouin

Auberge de L'Abbeye
12 place Guillaume le Conquerant
27800 Le Bec Hellouin
+33 2 32 44 86 02

Deauville

Normandy Barrière
38 rue Jean Mermoz
14804 Deauville
+33 2 31 98 66 22

Royal Barrière
Boulevard Cornuche
14804 Deauville
+33 2 31 98 66 33

Honfleur

Hôtel Ferme Saint-Simeon
Rue Adolphe-Marais
14600 Honfleur
+33 2 31 81 78 00

La Chaumière
Route du Littoral
14600 Honfleur
+33 02 31 81 63 20

Les Maisons de Lea
Place Sainte-Catherine
14600 Honfleur
+33 2 31 14 49 49

Manoir de la Poterie & Spa
Chemin Paul Ruel
141133 Honfleur
+33 2 31 88 10 40

Paris

Bel-Ami Hôtel
7–11 rue St-Benoît
75006 Paris
+33 1 42 61 53 53

Hôtel Balzac
6 rue Balzac
75008 Paris
+33 1 44 35 18 00

Hôtel Relais-Christine
3 rue Christine
75006 Paris
+33 1 40 51 60 80

Rouen

Hôtel Hermitage Bouquet
58 rue Bouquet
Rouen 76000
+33 2 32 12 30 40

References

www.thefrenchtable.com.au
www.chateau-life.com
www.australiansinfrance.com
www.atmyfrenchtable.com

Acknowledgements

Thank you to my publisher, Kirsten Abbott, for her faith and determination, and to Nikole Ramsay for her stunning photography and her friendship. Sincere thanks, too, go to Mark Roper for his incredible food photography, and to food stylist Leesa O'Reilly and home economist Deb Kaloper.

I thank all those at Penguin, especially John Canty and Bridget Maidment, whose tireless work made for such a beautiful book.

Thanks to Marieke Brugman, whose magic in the kitchen helped ensure such a successful first French Table.

I'm grateful to all our Aussie friends and family: Paul, Denise, Sarah, Jon and Alex Webster; Sally, Theo, Louis, Hendrik, Matilde and Beatrice Speelmans; the Harding family; Megan and Tony Rule; the Littlewoods; Louise Rice; Richard Taylor; Lisa and Martin James; Debra and Jon Sloane; Andrew Sellars-Jones; Alison Webster; Cynthia Mayes; Judy Beamish; Chase Jacabson; Anthony and Lisa Brown; Jeremy and Hamish Brown; Barbara Brown; Catherine and Sarah Barker; Geoffrey, Catherine and Nicole Hunter; Caroline Brand; Stephanie and David Holland; William Murray; Harrison and Justin Sloane; Harry and Zoe Prince; Lou and Phil Prince; Col and Beth Magik; Jacquie Naylor; and Ally and Gina Naylor. Without your visits and support, the journey would not have been as fun. Thanks to Lytlewode Press for all the magnificent artworks hanging in the chateau. www.lytlewode.com

And lastly, thanks to the most courageous kids alive – Lachie, Millie, Maddie and Alex. Your determination and sense of adventure make my heart sing.

The publishers would like to thank the following stockists for supplying materials for the food photography:

Stepback Antique Interiors: 103 Burwood Road, Hawthorn, Victoria, (03) 9815 0635
Market Import: 19 Morey Street, Armadale, Victoria, (03) 9500 0764
Exlibris Prints: 1060 High Street, Armadale, Victoria, (03) 9509 0900
    and 89 Vincent Street, Daylesford, Victoria, (03) 5348 1802
Sanders & King: 13 Morey Street, Armadale, Victoria, (03) 9500 1150
Izzi & Popo: 258 Ferrars Street, South Melbourne, Victoria, (03) 9696 1771
Milgate Fabrics: 533 High Street, Prahran, Victoria, (03) 9510 9811

Index

VIKING

Published by the Penguin Group
Penguin Group (Australia)
250 Camberwell Road, Camberwell, Victoria 3124, Australia
(a division of Pearson Australia Group Pty Ltd)
Penguin Group (USA) Inc.
375 Hudson Street, New York, New York 10014, USA
Penguin Group (Canada)
90 Eglinton Avenue East, Suite 700, Toronto, Canada ON M4P 2Y3
(a division of Pearson Penguin Canada Inc.)
Penguin Books Ltd
80 Strand, London WC2R 0RL England
Penguin Ireland
25 St Stephen's Green, Dublin 2, Ireland
(a division of Penguin Books Ltd)
Penguin Books India Pvt Ltd
11 Community Centre, Panchsheel Park, New Delhi – 110 017, India
Penguin Group (NZ)
67 Apollo Drive, Rosedale, North Shore 0632, New Zealand
(a division of Pearson New Zealand Ltd)
Penguin Books (South Africa) (Pty) Ltd
24 Sturdee Avenue, Rosebank, Johannesburg 2196, South Africa

Penguin Books Ltd, Registered Offices: 80 Strand, London, WC2R 0RL, England

First published by Penguin Group (Australia), 2008

3 5 7 9 10 8 6 4 2

Cover and text design by John Canty © Penguin Group (Australia)
Cover and author photographs by Nikole Ramsay
Food photography by Mark Roper, home economy by Deborah Kaloper,
food styling by Leesa O'Reilly on pages 93–99, 102, 109, 160–65,
169–72, 174, 226–43, 278–83, 286, 289–90, 292, 306, 309
Photography by Peter Webster on pages 105, 268 (bottom left), 303–4
Typeset in 12/18 Fournier by Post Pre-press Group, Brisbane, Queensland
Colour reproduction by Splitting Image, Clayton, Victoria
Printed and bound in China by 1010 Printing International Limited

National Library of Australia
Cataloguing-in-Publication data:

Webster, Jane.
At my French table : food, family and joie de vivre in a
corner of Normandy.
ISBN 978 0 670 07032 9
1. Webster, Jane. 2. Australians – France – Normandy –
Biography. 3. Normandy (France) – Description and travel.
4. Normandy (France) – Social life and customs. I. Title.

944.084092

penguin.com.au